"Now therefore ye are . . . built upon

the foundation of the apostles and prophets,

Jesus Christ himself being

the chief corner stone;

in whom all the building fitly framed

together groweth unto an holy temple in the Lord."

Ephesians 2:19–21

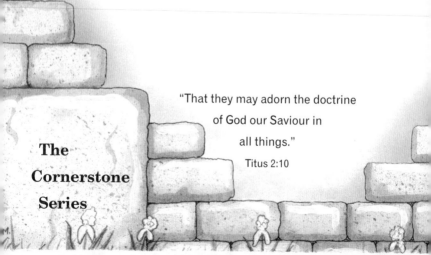

"That they may adorn the doctrine

of God our Saviour in

all things."

Titus 2:10

The Cornerstone Series

MORAL
PURITY

By Aaron M. Shank

Rod and Staff Publishers, Inc.
P.O. Box 3, Hwy. 172
Crockett, Kentucky 41413
Telephone (606) 522-4348

Cover Photo: © Photodisc by Getty Images

ISBN 0-7399-2400-1
Catalog no. 2336.3

1   2   3   4   5   —   16   15   14   13   12   11   10   09   08   07

CONTENTS

Introduction

Introduction

It was moral corruption that brought the judgment of God down on the earth in Noah's day. Holy Writ declares that "every imagination of the thoughts of [man's] heart was only evil continually." Noah and his family were an exception, however, and were spared the God-sent deluge that destroyed the world of their day. See Genesis 6–8.

It was moral corruption that brought fire and brimstone down from heaven on Sodom and Gomorrah, ushering Sodom's society suddenly into "suffering the vengeance of eternal fire." See Genesis 19 and Jude 7.

It was our Lord Jesus Christ from heaven who informed and forewarned us that "as it was in the days of Noe . . . also as it was in the days of Lot [the days of Sodom and Gomorrah] . . . even thus shall it be in the day when the Son of man is revealed" (Luke 17:26–30).

It can hardly be debated that the characteristically duplicated days of Noah and Lot are upon us today. The rapid increase of shamelessness in this generation related to perverted morals is appalling, to say the least. Could it have been more flagrant in Noah's and Lot's days?

This little volume is a frank discussion on (1) the principles of purity, (2) the perversions of purity, and (3) the provision for and protection from the spiritual and moral decadence of these last days. Although the message is frank, it is no more frank than the Holy Bible itself.

It is hoped that the frankness of these pages will help to preserve us from becoming calloused to the sensual atmosphere about us and will inspire some souls to "flee fornication" (1 Corinthians 6:18) and every other vile form of impurity. May it also motivate purity of heart and holiness of life, "without which no man shall see the Lord" (Hebrews 12:14).

"For the grace of God that bringeth salvation hath appeared to all men, teaching us that, denying ungodliness and worldly lusts, we should live soberly, righteously, and godly, in this present world; looking for that blessed hope, and the glorious appearing of the great God and our Saviour Jesus Christ; who gave himself for us, that he might redeem us from all iniquity, and purify unto himself a peculiar people, zealous of good works" (Titus 2:11–14).

—*Aaron M. Shank*

And now, little children, abide in him; that, when he shall appear, we may have confidence, and not be ashamed before him at his coming. . . . And every man that hath this hope in him purifieth himself, even as he is pure.

1 John 2:28; 3:3

1.

Principles of and Provisions for Moral Purity

I would like to start this treatise on moral purity in the Name of the one who is purity personified. Jesus Christ, the pure, sinless, spotless Son of God— the one who was never defiled by any contaminating influence—imparted purity to those who came in touch with Him and sensed their need of Him.

Once a Pharisee bade Jesus come into his house

and dine. A woman who was a sinner came in and wept before Jesus. As her tears fell on His feet, she softly removed them with her long hair. Then the Pharisee said within himself, "This man, if he were a prophet, would have known who and what manner of woman this is that toucheth him." Jesus promptly answered the Pharisee's thoughts and assured him that He Himself was not defiled through this contact, but that the contact really resulted in the cleansing and purifying of this sinful woman. Jesus was never contaminated with sin. Rather, He imparted purity (Luke 7:36–50).

THE HOLINESS OF GOD—
THE SINFULNESS OF MAN

Isaiah saw the holiness and purity of God. He heard the celestial beings acclaim that purity. "Holy, holy, holy, [Purity, purity, purity!] is the LORD of hosts." Purity and holiness may be considered synonymous terms. When Isaiah saw that vision of the purity of God, he said, "Woe is me! for I am undone." This was probably not Isaiah's initial experience in his calling as a servant of God. It was rather at the time of his calling to a special prophetic ministry to a morally corrupt people. As he envisioned the holiness of God, he sensed his own impurity and his own inadequacy.

He then cried out, "Woe is me! . . . because I am a man of unclean lips."

Who with a vision and concept of the purity of God would feel qualified to speak or write on the subject of purity? Isaiah did not consider himself qualified to go out and proclaim the holiness of God. But there was a provision for Isaiah. When he sensed his woeful inadequacy and his need of purity, one of the angels (perhaps one that had proclaimed the holiness and the purity of God) took a coal from off the altar, flew quickly, and cleansed the lips of Isaiah. He said, "Thine iniquity is taken away, and thy sin purged." Isaiah could now go and proclaim the holy demands of a holy and pure God. He was now, typically, "washed in the crimson flood, / Cleansed and made holy, humble and lowly, / Right in the sight of God."

The Hebrew word for *altar* means "an elevated place of slaughter." In Leviticus 1, the sacrifice was to be killed and the blood sprinkled on the altar. The sacrifice was to be skinned and then cut in pieces and burned on the altar. The altar of the Old Testament was a type of Calvary where Jesus was led "as a lamb to the slaughter." There He was bruised, broken, beaten, and lifted up to experience the consuming death of Calvary. The fire that the angel took from the altar to cleanse the lips and purge the iniquity of

11

Moral Purity

Isaiah, thus qualifying him to think and to proclaim the purity of God, was symbolic of the cleansing "fire" of Calvary and its effect on needy, sinful creatures in preparing them for the service of a holy God.

As we think of the purity of God and of our own failures and inadequacy, we experience a deep sense of unworthiness that makes us look to God for cleansing. We should experience a longing within our hearts to be partakers of the purity and holiness of God. Only then will we be ready to hear what God has to tell us and to share it with others.

By *purity* we mean "clean, untainted, unmarred by sin, and uncontaminated with evil."

The word *moral* in a broad sense refers to all matters of right and wrong, not just one phase or one type of wrongdoing. The Old Testament is said to contain the ceremonial law and the moral law. The ceremonial law had to do with the ordinances and ceremonies of the Old Testament times. The moral law had to do with the principles of purity and holiness of the Old Testament times. All principles of right and wrong set forth in the Law are considered the moral law of the Old Testament.

Generally, however, when we talk about moral purity or immorality, we associate it with sexual conduct. One dictionary definition for *moral* is "sexual virtue." When confessions are made by persons who have transgressed and fallen into sexual sin, such sin is often referred to as moral transgression. Usually when we talk about morality or immorality, we are referring more particularly to the purity or impurity related to sensual and sexual sins of the depraved nature.

The Bible teaches much against moral corruption. It records the history of a number of moral failures. The Bible also has standards, principles, and provisions for moral purity.

Mankind as a whole has increasingly degenerated into a morally corrupt society. The central theme of our Bible is redemption from impurity, and the supreme call of God's Word is the call to separation from moral impurity. The ultimate goal of our Bible is to bring us out of this sinful world and to bring us into the purity of God. That is the ultimate purpose of the Bible.

A basic Scripture for this message is found in 1 Thessalonians 4:1–8: "Furthermore then we beseech you, brethren, and exhort you by the Lord Jesus, that as ye have received of us how ye ought to walk and to please God, so ye would abound more and more. For ye know what commandments we gave you by the Lord Jesus. For this is the will of God, even your sanctification, that ye should abstain from fornication: that every one of you should know how to possess his vessel in sanctification and honour; not in the lust of concupiscence, even as the Gentiles which know not God: that no man go beyond and defraud his brother in any matter: because that the Lord is the avenger of all such, as we also have forewarned you and testified. For God hath not called us unto uncleanness, but unto holiness." (purity)

God has not called us to impure living or uncleanness, but unto holiness and purity. "He therefore that despiseth, despiseth not man, but God, who hath also given unto us his holy Spirit."

PRINCIPLES OF MORAL PURITY

Origin of

1. Moral purity originates with and issues from God. The passage quoted above says, "This is the will of God, even your sanctification." Moral purity comes from God. God wants us to be pure and to keep ourselves from impurity.

"As obedient children, not fashioning yourselves according to the former lusts in your ignorance: but as he which hath called you is holy, so be ye holy in all manner of conversation; because it is written, Be ye holy; for I am holy" (1 Peter 1:14–16).

Holiness and purity originate with and issue

14

from God, because God is the essence of purity. In Leviticus, God told His people a number of times that they should live by the standard that He gave them. And the reason He repeatedly gave for this command is that He, the Lord their God, is a holy God, and therefore, He called upon them to be a holy people.

God certainly knows what is right, because God is right. There is no flaw in God. "Holy, holy, holy." God is a God of perfection, and therefore He knows what the standards and principles of perfection are. They issue from God. "I am the LORD." "He . . . that despiseth, despiseth not man, but God."

Standard Permanently Established

2. The standard of moral purity is permanently established. This standard was established by God millenniums ago, and it remains unchanged today. We are living in a day when people say that the Bible is outdated. They say we have new ways of living and new lifestyles. They talk about a new morality. But the laws of moral purity established by God in His original Law remain unchanged. The new morality as emphasized in some circles today is really the old immorality.

If the Scriptures were being written today, they

would be written no differently than they are. The Bible will never become outdated or obsolete. When Peter and other writers of the Scriptures referred to the moral law of the Old Testament, which legislated against adultery, fornication, homosexuality, bestiality, and many other forms of indecency and impurity, they repeatedly reestablished those laws. "But as he which hath called you is holy, so be ye holy in all manner of conversation; because *it is written,* Be ye holy; for I am holy" (1 Peter 1:15, 16). The New Testament does not annul any of those standards, but rather, strengthens them. If there is a difference in the New Testament era, it is not in a *change* of standards, but it is in a *strengthening* of those standards (Matthew 5:27, 28).

In fact, the day in which we live is the most responsible day in which man has ever lived. The Bible says that they who died before the Law was given to Israel at Sinai perished unaccountable to that Law, or "without law," while those who died in the Law (or since the Law was given at Sinai) shall be judged by the Law. When Jesus sent the disciples out to preach, they were instructed that if people reject their message, it is going to be more tolerable for those who lived in the day of the destruction of Sodom (that was before the Law was given), than for those people who reject their message (Matthew 10:14, 15).

The Scriptures say that "he that despised Moses' law died without mercy under two or three witnesses: of how much sorer punishment, . . . shall he be thought worthy" who goes against the light in the New Testament era? See Hebrews 10:28, 29.

To summarize, we live in the most enlightened and therefore the most responsible era of all time. The standard is not lessened today. The standards of moral purity are permanently established.

In the last book of the Bible, we are told that "the fearful, and unbelieving, and the abominable, and murderers, and whoremongers, and sorcerers, and idolaters, and all liars, shall have their part in the lake which burneth with fire and brimstone: which is the second death" (Revelation 21:8).

A Priority With God

3. Moral purity is a priority with God. "As ye have received of us how ye ought to walk and to please God, so ye would abound more and more" (1 Thessalonians 4:1). James, in writing about the earthly wisdom, stated, "This wisdom descendeth not from above, but is earthly, sensual, devilish" (James 3:15). He then continued, "But the wisdom that is from above is *first pure*" (James 3:17). Moral purity is a

Moral Purity

priority with God for time and eternity. For eternity, God says, "He which is filthy, let him be filthy still: and he that is righteous, let him be righteous still" (Revelation 22:11).

From a Pure Heart

4. *The practice of moral purity must come from a pure heart.* "For this is the will of God, even your sanctification, that ye should abstain from fornication" (1 Thessalonians 4:3). What is sanctification? *Sanctification* is "a cleansing and a setting apart; a cleansing of the heart and a setting apart of that life for God." There must be an inner work of cleansing of the heart before an expression of holiness and purity can issue out of that heart. "Either make the tree good, and his fruit good; or else make the tree corrupt, and his fruit corrupt: for the tree is known by his fruit. O generation of vipers, how can ye, being evil, speak good things? for out of the abundance of the heart the mouth speaketh. A good man out of the good treasure of the heart bringeth forth good things: and an evil man out of the evil treasure bringeth forth evil things" (Matthew 12:33–35). There we have it. The practice of moral purity must issue from a heart of purity!

The psalmist wrote, "I was shapen in iniquity;

and in sin did my mother conceive me" (Psalm 51:5). The Bible teaches throughout that by nature we are sinful creatures. Our bent or tendency is to be sinful. A little boy was asked one time why we do not have to teach children to be naughty. His answer was, "I don't know unless we've just been born wrong." He was exactly right. We have all been born wrong. We go astray, naturally. Children do not have to be taught to be dishonest. They do not have to be taught to be morally impure. Sin is there by nature. That is the reason why we "must be born again" John 3:7).

Peter, acknowledging that our first birth was of corruptible seed, put it this way: "Being born again, not of corruptible seed, but of incorruptible, by the word of God, which liveth and abideth for ever" (1 Peter 1:23). Paul declared, "Therefore if any man be in Christ, he is a new creature: old things are passed away; behold, all things are become new" (2 Corinthians 5:17). What old things? Read the catalogs of sins in the New Testament, such as are found in 1 Corinthians 6:9, 10; Galatians 5:19–21; Ephesians 5:3–5; Colossians 3:5; and Revelation 21:8. All those sins belong to the old life. "If any man be in Christ, he is a new creature," and *purity* will issue out of a heart that is made pure. Purity of practice comes from purity of heart.

Moral Purity

A Growing Experience

5. *Moral purity, to be maintained, must be a growing experience.* The apostle Paul, making a plea for moral purity, wrote, "So ye would abound more and more." James wrote: "Purify your hearts, ye double minded" (James 4:8). The only way for us to maintain purity is to grow in our expressions of purity. We sing, *"More* like the Master" and *"Purer* in heart," meaning "I want to be purer than I have been."

In the last two verses of 2 Peter, the apostle wrote, "Ye therefore, beloved, seeing ye know these things before, beware lest ye also, being led away with the error of the wicked, fall from your own stedfastness. But grow in grace, and in the knowledge of our Lord and Saviour Jesus Christ" (2 Peter 3:17, 18). As long as we are growing in grace, we cannot fall from grace. It is when we stop growing in grace that we fall from grace. Moral purity cannot be maintained if it is not a growing experience. When we become satisfied with ourselves, we are no longer moving forward and are in danger of a downfall.

In Sharp Contrast to an Immoral World

6. *Moral purity, as the Scriptures portray it, is in sharp contrast to the corruptions of an immoral world.* The passage from 1 Thessalonians 4 states that "every

one of you should know how to possess his vessel in sanctification and honour; not in the lust of concupiscence, even as the Gentiles which know not God" (1 Thessalonians 4:4, 5). Not like the world. We shall not do as they do. Our lives should be in sharp contrast to the lives of the sinful society about us. We should not expect to be in line or in tune with the world. "Know ye not that the friendship of the world is enmity with God? whosoever therefore will be a friend of the world is the enemy of God" (James 4:4). And in that connection, James labeled the lovers of the world "adulterers and adulteresses." We are spiritual adulterers and adulteresses if we love the world and seek its approval and friendship rather than the approval and friendship of God.

One young man, who had a family and was ordained to the ministry, was talking to a neighbor about moral conditions in the world. Then they shared with each other the experiences of their courtship days. The neighbor shared his experiences first, and then the minister shared his method of conduct during his courtship. As he explained the carefulness that he and his friend (now his wife) exercised to keep themselves pure and to obey the Scriptural admonition, "It is good for a man not to touch a woman," the neighbor listened with keen interest.

21

Moral Purity

His response was, "That kind of conduct is out of this world." And it is. It *is* out of this world. "Wherefore come out from among them, and be ye separate, saith the Lord, and touch not the unclean thing; and I will receive you, and will be a Father unto you, and ye shall be my sons and daughters, saith the Lord Almighty. Having therefore these promises, dearly beloved, let us cleanse ourselves from all filthiness of the flesh and spirit, perfecting holiness in the fear of God" (2 Corinthians 6:17–7:1).

Separation—an Eternal Reality

7. This sharp moral contrast between the conduct of the godly and ungodly will be an eternal reality. "[Let] no man go beyond and defraud his brother in any matter: because that the Lord is the avenger of all such" (1 Thessalonians 4:6). "He which is filthy, let him be filthy still . . . and he that is holy, let him be holy still" (Revelation 22:11). This sharp contrast or cleavage will be an eternal reality. God will divide between the right and the wrong, between the pure and the impure. And there will be an eternal separation. Separation began back in the dateless past when the devil rose up against God, and it will go on into the dateless future. The separation between good and evil, purity and impurity, righteousness and unrighteousness will be eternal.

"And there shall in no wise enter into [the heavenly city] any thing that defileth, neither whatsoever worketh abomination. . . but they which are written in the Lamb's book of life" (Revelation 21:27).

PROVISIONS FOR ACHIEVING MORAL PURITY

The Holy Spirit

1. The Holy Spirit is provided to help us to become morally clean and to maintain moral purity. "He therefore that despiseth, despiseth not man, but God, who hath also given unto us his holy Spirit" (1 Thessalonians 4:8). God has given us His pure Spirit. There are many impure spirits in the world, but there is only one Holy Spirit.

God has sent the Holy Spirit into the world. He poured His Spirit out upon all flesh. The Holy Spirit is a restraining agent that keeps sin from coming to its climax in the world. He is a restraining power in the whole world.

The Holy Spirit comes to the individual who has sinned ("*all* have sinned" [Romans 3:23]) and begins to make him aware of his need. He speaks to his conscience: "You need something that you do not have. You are a sinner. You are condemned." The Holy Spirit then enables the one who responds to Him to look to God for help. He finally brings him to Jesus Christ, where he humbly confesses Christ and receives Him as his Saviour, Lord, and Deliverer. The Holy Spirit then becomes a guide to lead him in the way of holiness, and in purity of life.

The Holy Spirit is the general restrainer in the world, but He is also a special guide and restrainer to the children of God as He woos them on toward the eternal union with Jesus Christ. He keeps prompting us and making us feel uncomfortable when we do the wrong thing. But when we find forgiveness and cleansing again, He then comes with His comforting grace and abundant peace and joy, which inspires us to persevere in a walk of purity.

How thankful we ought to be for the presence of the Holy Spirit. We would never get through to glory if it were not for His convicting and correcting power. How quick we ought to be to recognize His chidings and proddings. Even the sincere Christian may at times discover a tendency in his own thinking or practice that is drawing him in the wrong direction. How does he discover this? The voice of the Holy Spirit interrupts and restrains by His convicting power. If that voice is heeded, the Spirit leads him on into purity and perfection in Jesus Christ. The work of the Holy Spirit in the world today is one of God's provisions to help us to be pure in heart and to be partakers of the nature of God and of His eternal glory. The psalmist realized his need of the Holy Spirit's help to have a clean heart and a right spirit, and he prayed, "Take not thy holy spirit from me" (Psalm 51:11).

Purity Through Cleansing

2. *We are pure through forgiveness and cleansing.* There is no such thing as moral purity without forgiveness, because "all have sinned, and come short of the glory of God" (Romans 3:23). We should face the fact that we have personally sinned and that we have a sinful nature which causes us to have a tendency to sin. If we do not understand and admit that we have personally sinned, and that we have a sinful nature, there is no salvation or forgiveness for us. "If we say that we have no sin [sin tendency], we deceive ourselves. . . . If we say that we have not sinned, we make [God] a liar" (1 John 1:8, 10). God makes us pure as He forgives and cleanses us through the merits of the blood of the Lord Jesus Christ. This is the salvation and purity that God has provided for us.

Moral Purity

The examples of forgiveness that we find in the Bible are very impressive indeed. They both provide a warning and are a source of great encouragement to us. God forgave Moses for his act of disobedience in smiting the rock instead of speaking to it. God forgave Samson for his disobedience through the subtility of a female enticer. His name appears in the list of heroes of faith and works in Hebrews 11.

One of the most outstanding examples of forgiveness is in the life of King David. David committed adultery, plotted the murder of Uriah, and connived a master cover-up for his sin. But there is no cover-up with God. "The eyes of the LORD are in every place, beholding the evil and the good" (Proverbs 15:3). "All things are naked and opened unto the eyes of him with whom we have to do" (Hebrews 4:13).

Both the magnitude of David's sin and the immeasurable mercy and forgiveness of God are absolutely astounding. When God exposed David's sin and the exceeding sinfulness of his sin through the prophet Nathan, the guilty king went down in deep contrition and cried out, "I have sinned against the LORD." When David made this confession, the prophet responded with some of the most gracious words in the Bible, "The LORD also hath put away thy sin; thou shalt not die" (2 Samuel 12:13). Why did David not need to die for his sin? Doubtless, the answer is found in the principle stated in Romans 5:20: "Where sin abounded, grace did much more abound." The testimony of David was "He hath not dealt with us after our sins; nor rewarded us according to our iniquities. For as the heaven is high above the earth, so great is his mercy toward them that fear him" (Psalm 103:10, 11). Just as the distance from earth to heaven is immeasurable, so mercy and grace from God is limitless for those who fear Him. Notice David's further testimony: "But the mercy of the LORD is from everlasting to everlasting upon them that fear him . . . ; to such as keep his covenant, and to those that remember his commandments to do them" (Psalm 103:17, 18). David's life was badly stained by moral corruption. The unpleasant memory of his sin followed him throughout his life; he also reaped a very bitter harvest. However, by genuine repentance and full confession, he was cleansed and made pure again through the forgiveness of God. His deep repentance and fullness of confession is found in several psalms of contrition.

In Psalm 32:4, David is very descriptive of his experience: "For day and night thy hand was heavy [in conviction] upon me: my moisture is turned into the drought of summer." And in verse 5 he wrote, "I acknowledged my sin . . . unto the LORD, and thou forgavest the iniquity of my sin." In Psalm 51:7, he testified that through God's cleansing, "I shall be whiter than snow." He never outlived the regrets of his moral failure, but he did enjoy a cleansing that made him just as pure as though he had never sinned.

The New Testament also speaks of being made pure through the magnitude of God's mercy and forgiveness. Writing to the church at Corinth, Paul reminded them that in the past some of them had been living in moral corruption such as fornication, adultery, effeminacy, and homosexuality, but that they were now washed and sanctified and justified. They were justified (just as though they had not sinned, in the sense of being guilty) "in the name of the Lord Jesus" and "by the Spirit of our God" (1 Corinthians 6:9–11).

The cleansing we receive for specific transgressions, and the cleansing we receive for those things we do that are wrong, but of which we are not aware, is all by the blood of Christ. Both the Old Testament and the New Testament teach this truth. David prayed, "Cleanse thou me from secret faults [the faults he was not aware of]. Keep back thy servant also from presumptuous [intentional] sins; . . . then shall I be upright, and I shall be innocent from the great transgression" (Psalm 19:12, 13). "If we walk in the light, as he is in the light, we have fellowship one with another, and the blood of Jesus Christ his Son cleanseth us from all sin [that we may not be aware of]. . . . If we confess our sins [that we know we have committed], he is faithful and just to forgive us our sins, and to cleanse us from all unrighteousness" (1 John 1:7, 9). To be cleansed from all unrighteousness is as pure as we can become. The sorrows, the regrets, and the unpleasant memories of sin can always be overpowered by the joy of forgiveness. We are pure through forgiveness.

The Word of God

3. *The Bible is given as a provision to help keep us pure.* The Word of God is food for the soul. How are we strengthened by it? Physically, we are strengthened by eating natural food. Spiritually, we have to eat the food of the Word to have strength. We do not know what temptations will come to us today. A good way to start the day is to nourish the soul and ask God to grant unto us the Holy Spirit's immediate help if we should face an emergency situation or if an unexpected test or temptation should be placed before us. We ought to be well nourished by the Word so that we will be strong. If we are undernourished when the test comes, we are in danger of failure.

Moral Purity

"Wherewithal shall a young man cleanse his way? by taking heed thereto according to thy word" (Psalm 119:9). The Bible is provided for our safety. Bible reading and meditation is vital to purity. "Meditate upon these things; give thyself wholly to them; that thy profiting may appear to all" (1 Timothy 4:15).

The following story from the *Star of Hope* illustrates the value of hiding God's Word in the heart for purity of thought and life, and for victory over enticement from evil sources.

A couple of men were going to try to lead a young man into sin, and offered him some wine to drink. They urged him to share with them in a little drinking party.

His answer was, "I thank you, sirs, but I never drink intoxicating beverages."

"Never mind, my lad, it will not hurt you. Come, have a drink with us."

Then this was his answer: "'Wine is a mocker, strong drink is raging: and whosoever is deceived thereby is not wise' " (Proverbs 20:1).

The men replied, "You don't need to be deceived. You won't necessarily be deceived if you drink just a little bit. You can control yourself."

The young man replied, " 'At the last it biteth like a serpent, and stingeth like an adder' (Proverbs 23:32), and I certainly think it wiser not to play with adders."

The men then tried to seduce him again, and the young man came back with, " 'If sinners entice thee, consent thou not' " (Proverbs 1:10).

In discussing between themselves their lack of success, one man said to another, "The fact is that the young man is so full of the Bible that we can't do anything with him."

What was the young man doing? He was using the Word of God to keep himself pure.

"THE BIBLE"

This Book is the mind of God. It reveals the state of man, the way of salvation, the doom of sinners, and the happiness of believers.

Its doctrines are holy, its precepts are binding, its histories are true, and its decisions are immutable. Read it to be wise, believe it to be safe, and practice it to be holy. It contains light to direct you, food to support you, and comfort to cheer you. It is the traveler's map, the pilgrim's staff, the pilot's compass, the soldier's sword, and the Christian's charter.

Moral Purity

Here paradise is restored, heaven opened, and hell disclosed. Christ is its grand object, our good its design, and the glory of God its end. Read it slowly, frequently, and prayerfully. Let it fill the memory, rule the heart, and guide the feet. It is a mine of wealth, a paradise of glory, and a river of pleasure. It is given you in life, will be opened in the judgment, and remembered forever. It involves the highest responsibility, will reward the highest labor, and will condemn all who trifle with its sacred contents.

—*Author Unknown*

Personal Diligence

4. Another provision that God has given us is a personal ability for personal application. We dare not miss this vital point in God's provision for purity. God made us with powers of cooperation, and He gave us the ability to use those powers. We are not spiritual robots. A vivid Scripture on our need for personal diligence in addition to God's supernatural provisions is found in 2 Peter 1:1–11.

Peter was addressing his message to Christians, who were possessors of the "precious faith . . . through the righteousness of God and our Saviour Jesus

Christ" (verse 1); who were recipients of multiplied "grace and peace . . . through the knowledge of God, and of Jesus our Lord" (verse 2); who were by "his divine power . . . given . . . all things that pertain unto life and godliness" (verse 3); who were resting in the "exceeding great and precious promises" of God (verse 4); who were "partakers of the divine nature" (New Birth); who had "escaped the corruption that is in the world through lust" (verse 4).

After presenting such a beautiful outline of the foundational principles of Christian experience, Peter adds the further requirements of personal diligence and personal effort which are needed to keep one from falling back into his old sins.

Beginning with verse 5, he wrote: "And beside this [beside the above-mentioned indispensable principles], giving all diligence, add to your faith virtue; and to virtue knowledge; and to knowledge temperance; and to temperance patience; and to patience godliness; and to godliness brotherly kindness; and to brotherly kindness charity."

Then he added two powerful little "ifs" in verses 8 and 10: "If these things be in you, and abound" (be in you in an active and practical way), your life will be fruitful and victorious, and "if ye do these things, ye shall never fall." He further states that this is what makes one's election with God sure, and warrants for him an abundant entrance into our Lord's eternal kingdom (verses 10, 11).

Joseph is a beautiful example of personal diligence in maintaining a life of purity. See Genesis 39:7–20. When he was under the persuasive influence of an enticer, the Bible says, "But he refused." His immortal words "How then can I do this great wickedness, and sin against God?" did not stop the persistent seducer. As she daily sought to allure him, "he hearkened not unto her to lie by her, or to be with her." Joseph finally fled from her presence. He gave all diligence to keep himself pure at all cost. In 1 Corinthians 6:18, Paul tells us to "flee fornication."

To maintain a life of purity requires personal application and diligence. It takes practical sanctification, not a mere profession of a "shouting" sanctification. *Practical sanctification* means "keeping clean in every area of life by personal application and good behavior." God has given us the power to cooperate with Him. He expects us to use that power. "Flee also youthful lusts: but follow righteousness, faith, charity, peace, with them that call on the Lord out of a pure heart" (2 Timothy 2:22).

Prayer and God's Keeping Power

5. God has given us the provision of prayer and His keeping power. Prayer often grows out of a sense of a need for supernatural help. Take time to pray. How can we be kept pure if we do not pray "unto him that is able to keep [us] from falling"? (Jude 24). We "are kept by the power of God" (1 Peter 1:5).

Personal application will never succeed without the power of God. God expects us to depend upon Him because without His supernatural help, our personal efforts will avail nothing. "Wherefore let him that thinketh he standeth take heed lest he fall" (1 Corinthians 10:12).

When Jesus prayed during what was possibly the greatest test of His earthly life, angels ministered unto Him. This brought the strength of heaven to Him for the test and for the task before Him.

Jesus said that we "ought always to pray, and not to faint" (Luke 18:1). The inference is that if we do not pray, we will faint. Paul wrote that we are to be "instant in prayer" (Romans 12: 12). That is, to pray immediately when there is a need. Paul also tells us to "pray without ceasing" (1 Thessalonians 5: 17) to never give up or stop praying.

Many beautiful prayer hymns that often speak to our own personal needs have been written and are

Moral Purity

included in our hymnbooks. Do your thoughts tend to wander in unwholesome channels? Sing "Come, gracious Spirit, heav'nly Dove, / With light and comfort from above; / Be Thou our guardian, Thou our guide, / O'er ev'ry thought and step preside." When sung sincerely, this song will give the mind a good spiritual bath.

Is temptation overwhelming you? Sing "I need Thee ev'ry hour, / Stay Thou near by; / Temptations lose their pow'r / When Thou art nigh." When we resist the tempter in this way, he will flee from us.

Do you feel that you are not living up to Christlike ideals or representing Him properly? Sing "Have Thine own way, Lord! Have Thine own way! / Hold o'er my being / Absolute sway! / Fill with Thy Spirit / Till all shall see / Christ only, always, / Living in me!"

There are many, many of these kinds of prayer hymns that should be memorized and be ready in the mind for instant use.

When you humbly depend on His keeping power, "God is faithful, who will not suffer you to be tempted above that ye are able [by personal effort and application]; but will with the temptation also make a way to escape [by supernatural help], that ye may be able to bear it" (1 Corinthians 10:13).

The Church

6. The church is provided to help us keep pure.
The faithful church is basically a pure society. The ultimate of purity will only be realized when we meet the Lord in the air and He presents the church without spot or wrinkle to God. The church is not infallible. She will need to continually battle against the spots and wrinkles in this world, but the true church as the body of Christ is the one organization on earth in which spots and wrinkles are taken care of until they are finally and completely done away with in the very presence of the spotless Lamb of God.

We need the church with her regular Sunday morning fellowship, special Bible conferences, revival meetings, prayer meetings, and Bible schools. In all these services, as the Bible is preached, taught, and meditated upon, we experience sanctification and cleansing "with the washing of water by the word" (Ephesians 5:26). Many service activities are also provided through the church, which help to strengthen and build us up in the faith. In faithfully assembling ourselves together, we are able "to provoke [stimulate one another] unto love and to good works" (Hebrews 10:24). The true church gatherings are the greatest gatherings that can be had on this side of eternity. All the activities of

37

the faithful church are designed to help us to be vessels unto honor, sanctified, and suitable for the Master's use (2 Timothy 2:21).

The apostle Paul warns us that there are sometimes dishonorable vessels in the great house (the church) who may exert a wrong influence. But there are also honorable vessels, like Joseph, Daniel, and Timothy in the Bible, who challenge us to be among those vessels unto honor.

I well remember an experience I had as a young teenager, sitting in church one night with other teenagers, a number of whom were dishonorable vessels. As we knelt for prayer, these young people used the occasion for a time of silly, frivolous entertainment and amusement. During their irreverent hilarity and laughter, a young man, just a bit older than I, suddenly refused to be entertained. Instead, he bowed his head, closed his eyes in reverence, and prayed. My reaction was "If he can do it, I can too." Years later, after I was grown and was ordained to the ministry, another ordained brother shared with me about a time when he and I were with a group of irreverent youth during prayer. When he saw me reverently close my eyes in prayer, he decided, "If he can do it, so can I." This was peer pressure in the right direction. Only God knows where this kind of peer pressure and influence will end.

Daniel's purpose of heart to stand for the principle of purity influenced his friends, and finally, through a decree from a world monarch, Daniel influenced the whole world to recognize his God.

When Paul wrote to young Timothy, he said, "Let no man despise thy youth; but be thou an example of the believers . . . in purity" (1 Timothy 4:12). Young people, as you take your stand and practice high standards of moral purity, you will exert peer pressure on other young people that may be greater than the influence of any other person in their experience. We never know the bounds of our influence. Young people, may you be a part of that provision by God and exert peer pressure in the right direction. In the "great house" of the church, be a vessel of gold and silver and precious stone; be that vessel "unto honour, sanctified, and meet for the master's use, and prepared unto every good work."

"Blessed are the pure in heart: for they shall see God" (Matthew 5:8).

Christ's Imminent Return

7. For those who are living for Jesus, the hope of His sure and sudden return is both a powerful incentive to constant purity and a solemn warning against even a

Moral Purity

moment of sinful thought or practice. Lest anyone
should yield to sin, presuming on the gracious forgiveness of God, we should be reminded that Jesus
never said, "Get ready for My coming again," but rather,
"Be ready." The five foolish virgins of Matthew 25:1–13
had been ready and waiting for the bridegroom, but at
the moment of his coming, their lamps were going out
and they were not able to enter in with those whose
lamps were trimmed and burning. Millions of people
will doubtless be indulging in impurities at the moment
Jesus comes, and the door will be closed with them on
the outside.

God will not give a seven-day notice or even ring
a five-minute bell, but "in such an hour as ye think
not the Son of man cometh" (Matthew 24:44).

"Take ye heed, watch and pray: for ye know not
when the time is. . . . Watch ye therefore: for ye know
not when the master of the house cometh, at even,
or at midnight, or at the cockcrowing, or in the morning: lest coming suddenly he find you sleeping. And
what I say unto you I say unto all, Watch" (Mark
13:33, 35–37).

"Precious Saviour, May I live
  Only for Thee,
Spend the powers Thou dost give
  Only for Thee,
Be my spirit's deep desire
  Only for Thee,
May my intellect aspire
  Only for Thee."

But fornication, and all unclean-ness, . . . let it not be once named among you, as becometh saints; nei-ther filthiness, nor foolish talking, nor jesting. . . . For this ye know, that no whoremonger, nor unclean person . . . hath any inheritance in the kingdom of Christ and of God.
Ephesians 5:3–5

2.

Perversions of Moral Purity

WHAT IS A PERVERSION?

A *perversion* is an act that goes counter to, or influences people to go counter to, that which is right. When Balaam was called by Balak to curse Israel (Numbers 22), God told him not to go. When Balak repeated his request to Balaam, and Balaam responded and was on his way, the angel of the Lord met him and told him that his way was perverse before the Lord. His perverted way was indicated by his asking counsel of the Lord the second time on something the Lord had forbidden him to do. When God speaks once against our doing something, that should be enough. When we go ahead and do something God tells us not to do, our way is perverse. When we ask God for a change in His original requirements or restrictions, He may allow us to go in a perverse way to our own hurt.

It is easy for our thinking to become perverted when we want to do that which we should not do. When the angel of the Lord stopped Balaam's donkey the third time, and Balaam in his madness had beaten the poor beast, the donkey supernaturally began to talk and reason with Balaam (2 Peter 2:15, 16). But Balaam was so perverse in his desire and so blinded that he could not see the angel or even be impressed with the supernatural way in which his donkey was talking to him. That donkey's example was a good object lesson of open-mindedness and obedience to the perverse and blinded Balaam.

If we were dealing with a horse, a mule, a cow, or any other beast, and it were to talk to us, I think we would sit up and take notice. We would probably be somewhat frightened and would pay close attention to what that beast had to tell us. But Balaam's way was so perverse that, instead of paying attention to the supernatural talking of his normally humble and obedient donkey, he told it that if he had his sword, he would kill it. One would think he would have been terribly afraid to threaten a talking donkey with death.

God's message of truth and purity to us today is just as supernatural as was the donkey's message to Balaam. Holy men wrote by inspiration of God. Those holy men gave us the supernatural message from a holy God. If we do not have a love for that supernatural message of holiness and moral purity, we may well become corrupt in our thinking and blinded and perverse in our ways.

When we are determined to take our own course against the course that God has prescribed, we finally get to the place where nothing convinces us or stops us in our perverted ways. We may actually get to the place where we think wrong is right and promote the wrong as being right. The apostle Paul refers to such people as those who have "changed the truth of God into a lie" (Romans 1:25).

The Bible contains a catalog of moral perversions, and it also tells us what constitutes moral purity. Furthermore, the Bible makes it clear that it is up to us to choose the type of life we will live. God said, "I have set before you life and death, blessing and cursing: therefore choose life" (Deuteronomy 30:19). In Ecclesiastes 11:9, young men are told, "Walk in the ways of thine heart, and in the sight of thine eyes: but know thou, that for all these things God will bring thee into judgment." We may choose the pleasures and the moral corruptions of this world, but in so doing we also choose the judgment of God upon us. We have the power of choice as it relates to the character of life we live and as it relates to the judgment of God upon us and to our eternal destiny.

Sometimes when moral perversions are specifically named, the accusation is made that this just puts ideas into people's minds and places a temptation before them. But the Bible is a fair book that sets before us what is right and what is wrong and then gives us the privilege and responsibility to make our choices. God did this for Adam and Eve, and He does it for us. To be forewarned should help us to be forearmed and to be spared from the "wages of sin [which] is death" (Romans 6:23).

In the end God will receive far more glory from a life that knows what is wrong and chooses the right than He could ever receive from a nonmoral creature that can make no choices.

We will now look at three basic areas in relation to perversions of moral purity.

SATAN'S SPECIAL PERSUASIVE INFLUENCE TO MORAL PERVERSIONS OF WHICH WE NEED TO BE AWARE

In Romans 1:32, following a description of in-depth moral perversions, the apostle Paul declares that the agents of moral corruption not only do these things, "but have pleasure in them that do them." Proverbs 4:16 informs us that the wicked "sleep not, except they have done mischief; and their sleep is taken away, unless they cause some to fall." In Proverbs 6:26, we are given another startling observation of the seduction of an immoral person: "For by means of a whorish woman a man is brought to a piece of bread: and the adulteress will hunt for the precious life." "The precious life" here undoubtedly means the pure life. Purity is precious in the sight of God and to those who practice purity. The adulteress will hunt for a pure person and seek to rob him of his precious purity and bring him "to a piece of bread" —a state of worthlessness.

In the seventh chapter of Proverbs, we are given some of the tactics of an agent of moral perversion in seeking and bringing to destruction a "precious life."

The chapter begins with the secret of protection from moral perversions (verses 1–5). An ardent love for God's holy commandments and laws of purity and a constant embracing of them will protect one from the type of strange seducer referred to in this chapter. The chapter ends with the tragedy of a ruined life that was unfortified and "void of understanding," doubtless because of a lack of appreciation for God's protecting laws.

Flattering Words

The first tactic mentioned is the use of flattering words (verse 5). Verse 21 describes further: "With her much fair speech she caused him to yield, with the flattering of her lips she forced him." Flattery often strikes a responsive chord on the part of "simple ones" (and sometimes on the part of intelligent ones) and opens the way for an effective, unwholesome influence.

Darkness

Another tactic was the use of the end of the day and the darkness of the night (verse 9). Jesus said that "men loved darkness rather than light, because their deeds were evil" (John 3:19).

Immodest Dress

The tactic of immodest dress—"the attire of an harlot" (verse 10)—is one of the great factors in the breakdown of resistance to moral perversions. Clothing made of bright colors, sheer materials, and patterns that are formfitting and that scantily cover the body might well be classified as the attire of an harlot, which is often a deadly tactic.

Physical Familiarity

Physical familiarity—the kiss and fondling each other (verses 13, 18)—tends to build up a sensual urge that sometimes causes one to lose control of his resistance to evil and to give way to indulgence in moral perversions. Physical intimacies between the sexes constitutes a preparation for that which belongs only to the married. "Can one go upon hot coals, and his feet not be burned?" (Proverbs 6:28).

The Religious Tactic

The religious tactic (verse 14) is often very subtly used in the enticing procedure of an enticer. In this context the adulterous person said, "I have peace offerings with me; this day have I paid my vows." She had a testimony of piety, of charity, and of religious loyalties. It has been said that "a show of piety sometimes becomes a shelter of iniquity," and we might add, "a *seduction* of iniquity." There have been many situations where an individual seeking the "precious life" used the religious approach in his deceptive seductions.

Several case histories could be cited in which men of perverted minds have approached pure young Christian women under the guise of spiritual interests, pretending to want help spiritually, only to bring their victims to moral disgrace, even to unwed motherhood. The disgrace, of course, is not in motherhood but in the acts preceding motherhood outside of marriage.

Persuasion

The final tactic used in Proverbs 7 was persuasion on the basis of seclusion and privacy in a setting conducive to lust and sexual stimulation (verses 16–20). Evil may be practiced in secrecy under the cover of darkness or behind locked doors as far as man is concerned, but we cannot hide from God, for "all things are naked and opened unto the eyes of him with whom we have to do" (Hebrews 4:13).

The tragic result of the above tactics was a ruined, fallen, unhappy victim of moral perversion (verses 22, 23). A "precious life" was sought for, found, and ruined by an adulterous woman.

"All Is Going Fine So Far"

The description of this young man "void of understanding" reminds one of the story of the man who jumped out of the tenth story of a building. As he went by each story, he said, "All is going fine so far." Too many young people play with impurity and try to assure themselves that all is going fine so far, but do not think of how crushing and bitter the end of the drop will be. As Samson played with his enticer (Judges 16), in essence he said a number of times, "All is going fine so far." But what a crushing blow he experienced at the end of his drop.

Motion Picture Industry

One of the most influential agencies in the world today promoting moral perversion is the motion-picture industry. To excite and captivate a morally degenerate society, the industry seems to know no limits in developing and portraying sensual scenes. One of the most morally corrupt and blasphemous movies, featuring Satan fathering a child through the influence of a witch, was among the top fifty all-time hits in the industry. Millions of dollars were spent by Americans to view this production in the first few months of its showing. Now the news media informs us of a recent movie production portraying our Lord Jesus Christ, the spotless, holy, harmless, and undefiled Son of God as both being married and committing adultery involving some of the holy women of the New Testament. To add to the perverting influence of this production, the developer declares that producing this movie is his way of trying to get closer to God.

We cry out like the martyrs of Revelation 6:10: "How long, O Lord, holy and true, dost thou not judge" the ungodly "and avenge" our precious Lord Jesus for such blasphemy against Thy beloved, holy Son, in whom Thou art well pleased? Although the movie industry may provide some wholesome, educational movies at times, the industry is basically corrupt and must be avoided for the sake of moral purity.

Public School Sex Education

Perhaps of equal influence in corrupting the morals of society in general is the sex education program of the public schools. The public schools' sex education is claimed to be basically on the prevention of sexual diseases, the prevention of conception, and the practice of abortion when conception takes place. This kind of education, doubtless, promotes— more than it prevents—perverted social activity. When these classes ignore or bypass moral purity as the one sure method of controlling sexual diseases and conception, they simply contribute to the same condition that existed in Noah's time when "every imagination of the thoughts of his [man's] heart was only evil continually" (Genesis 6:5). This duplication of the corruption of Noah's time exists today as a sign of the last days before the coming of Jesus and the destruction of the world.

Books, Magazines, Pictures

Printing presses are turning out hundreds of tons of books, magazines, and leaflets which pervert the minds and morals of millions. These pornographic materials are scattered all over the country and are sometimes even dropped along highways and picked up by unsuspecting persons. If or when this happens, the only place these materials should find is the fire (Acts 19:19).

God gave specific commandment to Israel to destroy the pictures they found in the land of Canaan when they would conquer the land (Numbers 33:50–52). Because of their powerful appeal to the sexual nature of man, advertising agencies have capitalized on the use of sensual pictures and statements to captivate the mind and promote the sale of their wares. Radio, television, and the Internet are also among the world's worst moral corrupters and morality killers.

The psalmist realized the danger of things like

this when he declared, "I will set no wicked thing before mine eyes: I hate the work of them that turn aside; it shall not cleave to me" (Psalm 101:3). In Deuteronomy 7:26, Moses commanded, "Neither shalt thou bring an abomination into thine house, lest thou be a cursed thing like it: but thou shalt utterly detest it, and thou shalt utterly abhor it; for it is a cursed thing."

Sensual Music

We should not overlook the perverting effects of the world's sensual music on the morals of society. In many places, children at a very early age are being bombarded by obscenity and violence through perverted music. Studies show that the average teenager of today listens to rock music four hours a day and that one-third of rock productions extol the vilest expressions of moral corruption and Satanism. Rock lyrics also glamorize drug and alcohol use, glorify rebellion to authority, and promote violence, self-destruction, and even suicide.

To ensnare and pervert unsuspecting souls, rock producers often put a Gospel message to their satanic music. One heavy metal rock-singing group of four men who appear in demonic fashion sing "So many bands give the devil all the glory—It's hard to understand. We want to change the story." They also say, "The number one thing for us is to tell the people about Jesus—especially the young kids—in a way they can understand."

One of the tricks of the devil is to take something that is basically good, like music, and turn it into a devilish device. Demonic music is one of Satan's chief tools for captivating and perverting the minds and morals of the world today.

The foregoing examples are some of Satan's agents or avenues for moral perversion. Doubtless, there are many, many more satanic ways he uses to influence and corrupt people's minds in his opposition to God and moral purity. "Be sober, . . . your adversary, the devil, as a roaring lion, walketh about, seeking whom he may devour" (1 Peter 5:8).

SOME SPECIFIC PRACTICES OF MORAL PERVERSION TO FLEE FROM

God, who is the ultimate, the last word in purity, has a right to identify the expressions of moral corruption from which we are to flee and over which we are to be victorious.

The Bible from cover to cover gives us many descriptive terms of moral impurity and much teaching and warning against it. The Bible also gives us examples of those who practiced impurity. In presenting these things, the Bible is not a suggestive book, but a book of enlightenment, warning, and deliverance. The real purpose of these exposures is to make us feel like fleeing from and abstaining from, rather than practicing, impurity. When God gave the command to not eat of the tree of the knowledge of good and evil, He was not suggesting to Adam and Eve that they partake of the tree, but was enlightening them on what would happen if they did so, so that they would not unknowingly bring untold damage to themselves and to their posterity. For the same reason, God tells us what the moral perversions are, and that they displease Him and result in His judgment on those who do such things. Following are some specific moral perversions on which the Bible enlightens us.

Adultery

1. Adultery is sexual involvement of a married person with anyone other than his or her marriage companion. Adultery is a term often used in the Bible. The first definite mention of this moral perversion is found in the Ten Commandments. In Exodus 20:14, God said, "Thou shalt not commit adultery." In the Old Testament times when those among God's people were guilty of this sin, they were to be put to death.

Leviticus 20:10 declares that "the man that committeth adultery with another man's wife, . . . the adulterer and the adulteress shall surely be put to death." In the New Testament, adultery is listed along with other detestable sins that bar people from the kingdom of God (1 Corinthians 6:9, 10). In Hebrews 13:4, we are told that God will judge "whoremongers and adulterers."

The Whoremonger

2. A whoremonger is a person who commercializes or sells the use of the body for sinful gratification in sexual perversions. In Revelation 21:8, whoremongers are listed among those who "shall have their part in the lake which burneth with fire and brimstone."

Divorce and Remarriage

3. Divorce and remarriage is a form of adultery that is overlooked by society in general today. Marrying or living with another partner while the original marriage partner is living is both an act and a continuous state of adultery. When Jesus was on earth, He restored the original divine plan of marriage, which was for one man and one woman to be joined in a bond as long as they both shall live (Mark 10:2–9). In authentic, clear, and positive words, Jesus declared, "Whosoever putteth away his wife, and marrieth another, committeth adultery: and whosoever marrieth her that is put away from her husband committeth adultery" (Luke 16:18). The Greek word for *committeth* means "action going on." Clearly, Jesus taught that persons involved in such a relationship live in a state of adultery. See also Romans 7:2, 3 and 1 Corinthians 7:39. Jesus said of marriage: "What therefore God hath joined together, let not man put asunder" (Mark 10:9). Over one million divorces in America annually means that man is putting asunder more than two million marriage partners every year—something that God says shall not be done. Most of these divorced persons marry another person. Such a relationship is nowhere sanctioned in the New Testament. Millions of Americans today are therefore living in this kind of adultery. Just because the state issues a license for a second marriage does not make this kind of socially acceptable adultery acceptable with God.

Fifty years ago divorce and remarriage was generally considered a disgrace in our country. In a recent article in the *U.S. News & World Report*, entitled "Why So Many Marriages Fail," the writer stated that divorce no longer carries the stigma it used to carry and that "there is no way, for example, that Ronald Reagan could have been elected president in 1960." In 1964 Nelson Rockefeller sought nomination of his party for the presidency of the United States, but was rejected because he had just recently been divorced and remarried. That was not very long ago.

Shortly after Edward VIII inherited the throne of England in 1936, he fell in love with Wallis Simpson, an American divorcee from Baltimore. His government refused to give its consent to his marriage to her and thus have a divorced woman become queen of their nation. King Edward VIII would not give up his interest in Wallis Simpson and so abdicated the throne and was married to her in 1937. In this disgraced relationship, he went into self-imposed exile in France for several years.

The above illustrations represent national concepts outside the realm of the Christian church. We believe that the strong position of the churches against divorce and remarriage at that time helped to establish this kind of conscience for the world. We are told that when John Jacob Aster was divorced in 1912 and wanted to remarry, he had difficulty finding a preacher who would perform the ceremony. Although he was an extremely wealthy man, he had difficulty finding a minister that would allow himself to be disgraced by marrying a couple involved in divorce. But finally, through an offer of twenty-five thousand dollars (a huge sum for those days), he got a preacher to marry him in his divorced state. However, that minister suffered so much disgrace over what he had done that he resigned his ministry. John Jacob Aster and his new bride were on the Titanic and were among those who sank with the wrecked vessel.

But things like the above do not happen today. That kind of stigma on divorce and remarriage has been largely lifted in the society of our day. It is becoming easier and easier to obtain a divorce. In fact, there are certain states that now offer no-fault divorce and a do-it-yourself divorce. But the standards of Almighty God do not change.

The blame for this change of attitude must be, at least in a large measure, placed on the professed church. The church constitutes a "conscience" for society in general. When the churches open their doors to receive into their fellowships divorced and remarried people, they are dulling the conscience of society on the issue and are accelerating the evils of divorce and remarriage. The result is a breakdown of the conscience of society on this evil and on moral purity in general.

The Woman-domination Movement

4. Another area of moral perversion is the woman-domination movement of our day. Actually, women's efforts for prominence and predominance in public life in many situations are moral issues, signs of moral corruption. With a news item in the May 22, 1984, issue of the *Gospel Herald,* a woman was pictured in a uniform on the stand before an address system. Her name is Virginia Mullencott, keynote speaker at the Seventh Women Ministry Conference held at Harrisonburg, Virginia. She was a professor of English at William Patterson College in New Jersey.

Registrants at the conference, held May 3–6, numbered close to two hundred. In attendance were women from as far away as California and British Columbia. Female pastors and women involved in various church agencies and activities were there. Three major addresses on the theme "In the Image of God" were presented by the keynote speaker. Mullencott is known as an Episcopalian theologian. (A theologian is one who teaches about God and the Bible in general.) She is the author of *Women, Men,* and other books. Nothing is said in this report but what is complimentary about this woman's addresses at this particular conference.

However, a few weeks later a "Readers Say" contributor wrote to the *Gospel Herald* because he was quite concerned about the fact that everything that was reported in the *Gospel Herald* about her ministry at the conference was favorable. He writes: "Recently at the Seventh Women Ministry Conference, Mullencott, an Episcopalian woman, planted several seeds which will surely spoil the crop if we let them go undetected. Since the *Gospel Herald* gave her a favorable report . . . I thought your readers should hear the rest of the story.

"Ms. Mullencott has a new revelation of God as a female. She said, 'God is our mother eagle, and we can put our trust in her.' She believes that the Bible authors added many of their own ideas and cultural hang-ups. . . . Ms. Mullencott taught that the church leaders are exploiting and oppressing the women, but the time is ripe for the women to grab the power. She said: 'These references to God as female as well as male, also remind women to get busy and take on whatever spiritual leadership roles they may be gifted toward.'

"Her view on marriage is that the church should accept and bless trial marriages, remarriages, people living together, and unions between people of the same sex. None of these need to be legally married or sanctioned by the church as long as they covenant together. She also said: 'Beautiful and supportive mutual relationships have been sustained both in marriage and without the benefit of the clergy between two men, two women, or people who are not married to each other.' (Tapes are available to verify this.)

"In her book, *Is the Homosexual My Neighbor?* she says that homosexuality is not sin and that the church should now ordain homosexuals."

This constitutes and illustrates for us a moral perversion.

Fornication

5. Fornication is the term usually used in the Bible to designate sexual permissiveness between those who are unmarried. Society in general today has become insensitive to the Bible teaching against this sin. A leading national magazine informs us that about one million unmarried teenage girls become expectant mothers annually in America. With all the conception-control methods of today, these people probably represent only a proportion of those who sin in this way. About one-half million of these will add to the sin of fornication by having abortions. The sin of destroying new life through abortion is often a consequence of the sin of fornication or adultery. Part of the reason for the fire and brimstone destruction of Sodom and Gomorrah was that they were "giving themselves over to fornication." "Giving themselves over" suggests that they no longer exercised any moral restraint or had any conscience against sexual perversions. They were giving full liberty to their sensual desires.

To teenagers and to all unmarried persons: "This is the will of God, . . . that ye should abstain from fornication" (1 Thessalonians 4:3).

"Flee fornication" (1 Corinthians 6:18).

Abortion

6. *The means of abortion to voluntarily terminate life, which is legalized by the nation and practiced so freely today, might well be listed with the moral perversions of society.* An estimated 1.5 million legal abortions were performed in the United States in the year 1980. The prospective mothers were mainly young, white, and unmarried. It is indeed a strange thing how protective people are toward beasts and birds and creeping things and yet have no regard for the sanctity of human life.

In his 1983 essay now in book form, *Abortion and the Conscience of the Nation,* President Ronald Reagan gives the information that, in the previous ten years, 15 million unborn children had had their lives snuffed out by legalized abortion. He then points out that this is ten times the number of all American casualties in all the American wars in the history of the nation. Think of it! Ten times as many lives taken in infanticide as have been lost in all the wars of America! One wonders how long God will withhold His judgment on a nation that has become so self-destructive through the practices of moral perversions.

Homosexuality and Lesbianism

7. *Homosexuality and lesbianism are moral perversions in which persons of the same sex become involved with each other in sexual gratification.* The Bible places these perversions under the disapproval and judgment of God. See Leviticus 18:22; 20:13; Romans 1:26–28; and 1 Corinthians 6:9–11. In the references in Leviticus, these sins were said to be an abomination to God and were punishable by death. In Romans 1:28, we are told that God gives such people "over to a reprobate mind, to do those things which are not convenient." In 1 Corinthians 6, it is stated emphatically that such persons "shall not inherit the kingdom of God." Some theologians today are changing "the truth of God into a lie" (Romans 1:25) in connection with these sins. One church leader writes in

his church's official paper, the *Gospel Herald:* "Homosexuality is of unknown origin, for which no one can be blamed." Another acclaimed theologian is quoted as saying "Homosexuality is not a sin," again changing the truth of God into a lie.

In 1 Corinthians 6:9–11, the apostle addresses people who *were* guilty of these filthy perversions, but who are *now* delivered by being washed, sanctified, and justified "in the name of the Lord Jesus, and by the Spirit of our God." The practice of homosexuality was another reason for which God showered fire and brimstone on the people of Sodom. The Bible never allows for homosexuality as a practice "for which no one can be blamed." Those practicing these things must be delivered and cleansed to escape the torments of the eternal fire to come. And praise God, deliverance is possible!

Bestiality

8. *Bestiality is the vulgar perversion of being sexually involved with beasts.* In Leviticus 18:23, 29 and 20:15, the Old Testament Law called for the death of both the involved person and the beast, thus indicating the vileness of such deeds and the judgment of God upon them.

Incest

9. Incest is the term used for the situation in which persons become involved sexually with immediate family members other than the marriage partners. In Leviticus 20:17 and 19, persons guilty of incest were to be put to death "in the sight of their people."

Self-abuse (Uncleanness)

10. Self-abuse, or masturbation, sometimes termed as solitary vice, while not specifically named in the Scriptures, may well be included in the term uncleanness. Uncleanness is listed along with other moral perversions in Galatians 5:19: "adultery, fornication, uncleanness, lasciviousness"; and in Colossians 3:5: "fornication, uncleanness, inordinate affection." Many other Scriptures that describe and warn against moral perversions include the term *uncleanness.* See Romans 1:24; 6:19; Ephesians 5:3, 5; 1 Thessalonians 4:7; and 2 Peter 2:10. Those who practice self-abuse live under a guilt complex that hinders their spiritual growth and usefulness.

When Jude wrote that Sodom and Gomorrah were "giving themselves over to fornication," he added, "and going after strange flesh" (Jude 7). Perhaps it could be said that all those who are involved in any deviation from moral purity are "going after strange flesh." The pure in heart who shall see God (Matthew 5:8) have come out from the world and have "escaped the corruption that is in the world through lust" (2 Peter 1:4).

Mind Perversion

11. Mind perversion is referred to numbers of times in the Bible in such terms as "vile affections," "vain . . . imaginations," "foolish heart," "lasciviousness," "inordinate affection," "without natural affection," "lust one toward another." See Romans 1:21, 26, 27, 31; Ephesians 4:19; and Colossians 3:5. In Matthew 5:27 and 28, our Lord teaches that the look of lust constitutes thought adultery and makes one guilty of moral perversion. Job said, "I made a covenant with mine eyes" (Job 31:1). The eye gate, if not disciplined, will open the heart gate to all kinds of corruption.

THE SEVERE PENALTIES OF MORAL PERVERSION TO BE SPARED FROM

In an article published in a national monthly magazine, entitled "The Slavery of Sex Freedom," the author wrote what happened after World War 1. Social counselors began to advocate sexual freedoms, free love, and the things that the nation is now engaging in without any shame. "Were they ashamed when they had committed abomination? nay, they were not at all ashamed, neither could they blush" (Jeremiah 8:12). The writer of the article called it the *slavery* of sex freedom. Among other things, he wrote that there are more nervous breakdowns, more murders, more suicides, more tears, and more unhappiness resulting from what people call sex *freedom* than from perhaps any other sinful practice of society.

One young girl who had become a slave of the so-called sex freedom, in describing her experience, said, "One word will describe it all: unhappiness." A number of years ago, Dr. Max Rafferty, in an article circulated throughout the nation about smut salesmen declared that "sexual misconduct is behind half the murders and most of the acts of violence committed in this country."

The advocates of sexual freedom contend that men and women will be happy with no restraints. But it does not turn out that way. It carries penalties with it. Proverbs 6:32, 33 warns, "Whoso committeth adultery with a woman lacketh understanding: he that doeth it destroyeth his own soul. A wound and dishonour shall he get; and his reproach shall not be wiped away." Here we are warned of the penalties of wounds, dishonor, reproach, and destruction of the soul.

Thank God, we can enjoy forgiveness, cleansing, and deliverance. And the joy of forgiveness can always overpower the regrets of transgression. But what kind of frame of reference will go with one through life? As Solomon wrote, "His reproach shall not be wiped away" (Proverbs 6:33). Then he continued in verses 34 and 35, "For jealousy is the rage of a man: therefore he will not spare in the day of vengeance. He will not regard any ransom; neither will he rest content, though thou givest many gifts." The writer of Proverbs is warning that there is no limit to the price or penalty that a man can put on another man for involving his wife in the violation of moral purity. There is no limit.

Unlimited Penalty

When I was a boy at home, there was a man who had a bakery route in my hometown of Annville, Pennsylvania. This man owned a house in town which he had rented to one of his customers. The owner began to socialize with the woman of the house in a rather suggestive manner. She and her husband agreed to play along with him. Finally, the baker was caught in the house in adulterous conduct. Her husband, who was supposed to be gone, suddenly appeared on the scene. He pretended to be in a rage and threatened to sue the invader.

The baker wanted to know what he could do to settle matters. The man of the house said, "You can deed me this property." Proverbs 6:34 indicates that there is no limit to the penalty that a man can put on one who gets involved with his wife in moral misconduct.

Incurable Diseases

Another penalty of moral perversion relates to sexually transmitted diseases. Of the adulterous woman in Proverbs 7:26, it is stated, "She hath cast down many *wounded:* yea, many strong men have been *slain* by her." Earlier in the chapter, speaking of her enticed victim, it is stated, "He goeth after her straightway, as an ox goeth to the slaughter, or as a fool to the correction of the stocks; *till a dart strike through his liver;* as a bird hasteth to the snare, and knoweth not that *it is for his life*" (verses 22, 23). These verses may refer to spiritual and moral damage done, or they may, and probably do, refer to physical damage done through contagious venereal diseases.

These diseases attack the skin, internal organs, bones, brains, eyes, nervous system, and the immune system, sometimes resulting in blindness, insanity, or even death. Proverbs 5:11 sums it up this way for the victims of moral perversion: "And thou mourn at the last, when thy flesh and thy body are consumed."

Syphilis and gonorrhea have long been known as dreaded venereal diseases which have disastrous results. From time to time medical science comes up with a "miracle drug" that may control the disease, but no really curative product has been found to wipe out venereal disease entirely. On the contrary, new diseases continue to attack and destroy the victims of immorality.

One of the most recently discovered and frightening diseases of our time is the disease called AIDS. AIDS is short for *A*cquired *I*mmune *D*eficiency *S*yndrome. This disease is contagious and is spread chiefly, although not only, through perverted moral conduct. AIDS destroys the body's God-given, built-in, normal resistance to disease.

It is only in recent years that AIDS has been identified and diagnosed. By the year 1988, there were 40,000 known deaths from the disease. Although the government and medical science are spending millions of dollars in research to find a medical remedy, there is no known medical cure available. The victims usually experience a slow, lingering, and sometimes miserable death.

In a national weekly news magazine for the week of January 29, 1990, an article on AIDS gives the following information that the national commission on AIDS reported a month earlier:

"Far from being over, the epidemic is reaching crisis proportions. . . . It will be much worse in the 1990s than in the 1980s."

Projections and estimates may vary and may not always represent reality, but they do give us a little idea of what those who study the situation think.

This article reports that "the Hudson Institute, a conservative think tank, says there are now 1.9 million to 3 million people infected. . . . Hudson projects that by 2002 the number of people infected could rise to nearly 15 million if there is no significant medical breakthrough and *if behavior changes do not occur* [emphasis ours]." Many other projecting institutions do not place the figure that high.

Presently in New York City, AIDS patients fill one in every twelve beds, at the cost of $1 million a day.

The article concludes by saying that "despite all that has been learned, the true extent of the AIDS threat remains unknown."

As old diseases are medically suppressed, new diseases seem to appear on the scene. Quite recently a national weekly news magazine carried an article on its medicine page under the caption "Another Sexual Blight to Fight." The article quotes a doctor as saying about HPV (a blight caused by the human papillomavirus) that "the virus is rampant," and "if it weren't for AIDS, stories about it would be on the front page of every newspaper." The disease is described as "sometimes painful and often incurable." Another news magazine in an article on the same subject estimated 500,000 new cases annually.

These diseases, which are almost exclusively related to and spread by acts of moral perversion, are a part of the severe penalties for the violations of moral purity. Some of these diseases do affect the newly born; so might it be that Sodom and Gomorrah, who were "giving themselves over to fornication, and going after strange flesh" had become so disease ridden when God destroyed them with fire and brimstone that they were no longer physically or morally fit to propagate their own race? Malachi 4:1 foretells of a time to come when God will again burn up the wicked and leave them neither root nor branch, that is, God will leave none of them to continue propagating their race.

Eternal Punishment and Suffering

The final and most severe of the penalties for moral impurities that are not repented of, forsaken, and cleansed by the blood of Christ is eternal separation from God and eternal suffering in the lake of fire: "But the fearful, and unbelieving, and the abominable, and murderers, and whoremongers, and sorcerers, and idolaters, and all liars, shall have their part in the lake which burneth with fire and brimstone: which is the second death" (Revelation 21:8).

This eternal separation will involve not only eternal punishment, but will also be a separation from all fleshly desires. The pleasures of sin are but for a season. "The world passeth away, and the lust thereof: but he that doeth the will of God abideth for ever" (1 John 2:17). Lustful, licentious, and loose living will not be practiced in hell.

In Ephesians 5:3–7, where Paul lists a number of immoral acts, he declares that "because of these things cometh the wrath of God upon the children of disobedience." Those who engage in immoral acts are "children of disobedience" to God's holy standards of purity.

There are so-called theologians who teach that once a person is saved, his relationship with God cannot be broken by "unworthy conduct." One such preacher assured his audience that "you can be living in adultery and be on your way to heaven." Then he added, "Of course, we don't recommend that."

Moral Purity

Another one wrote, "Neither sin nor death can destroy a relationship that is eternal." This kind of teaching constitutes "turning the grace of our God into lasciviousness" and contributes to carelessness and indulgence in moral perversions.

Paul was addressing Christians when he declared, "If ye live after the flesh, ye shall die" (Romans 8:13) and "If any man have not the Spirit of Christ, he is none of his" (Romans 8:9).

John stated clearly that our eternal life is in God's Son and that "he that hath the Son hath life; and he that hath not the Son of God hath not life" (1 John 5:12). When one engages in acts of moral impurity, he cannot claim to have the Son of God nor the Spirit of Christ in his life. He rather has the spirit of the children of disobedience. When Christ, who is our life, goes out of our life, eternal life goes with Him. Our eternal life is in the Son and is therefore in us only when we have the Son in us. Paul also declared that "Christ in you" is our only "hope of glory" (Colossians 1:27). John further warned, "Little children, let no man deceive you: he that doeth righteousness is righteous, even as he is righteous" (1 John 3:7). God has provided a way for us to be spared from the penalties of unhappiness, disease, death, and eternal punishment.

"Keep Thyself Pure"

The Biblical appeal "Keep thyself pure" is the way to avoid the emotional, the physical, and the eternal penalties that come upon those who indulge in moral perversions. Purity of heart is possessed through repentance, forgiveness, and cleansing by the blood of Christ, and through a personal purpose of heart with perseverance in principles of right.

"If we walk in the light, as he is in the light, we have fellowship one with another, and the blood of Jesus Christ his Son cleanseth us from all sin" (1 John 1:7).

THE BIRD
WITH A
BROKEN PINION

I walked through the woodland meadows,
    Where sweet the thrushes sing,
And I found on a bed of mosses
    A bird with a broken wing.
I healed its wound, and each morning
    It sang its old sweet strain;
But the bird with a broken pinion
    Never soared as high again.

I found a young life broken
    By sin's seductive art;
And, touched with a Christlike pity,
    I took him to my heart.
He lived with a noble purpose,
    And struggled not in vain;
But the life that sin had stricken
    Never soared as high again.

But the bird with a broken pinion
    Kept another from the snare,
And the life that sin had stricken
    Raised another from despair.
Each loss has its compensation;
    There is healing for every pain;
But the bird with the broken pinion
    Never soars as high again.
                —*Hezekiah Butterworth*

Blessed are the pure in heart: for they shall see God.
            Matthew 5:8

Keep thyself pure.
            1 Timothy 5:22

Wash me, and I shall be whiter than snow.
            Psalm 51:7

3.

Proper Expressions of Purity

The title suggests that we should *practice* moral purity. If we believe in a principle, we must believe in an expression of it. "Even so faith, if it hath not works, is dead, being alone" (James 2:17). If a principle does not result in a practical expression, it is either dead or dying.

Christianity begins on the inside and works out. Jesus and the apostles taught this. "I beseech you therefore, brethren, by the mercies of God, that ye present your bodies a living sacrifice, holy, acceptable unto God, which is your reasonable service. And be not conformed to this world: but be ye transformed by the renewing of your mind" (Romans 12:1, 2).

Mind, heart, and spirit are often used synonymously in the New Testament and represent the inner life of our being. When the mind is renewed, the inner life is renewed and transformed. Outward expressions of purity follow the inner work of purity.

PROPER EXPRESSIONS

The apostle Paul wrote to Timothy, "Keep thyself pure" (1 Timothy 5:22). Keep on practicing purity. John wrote, "Every man that hath this hope in him purifieth himself, even as he is pure" (1 John 3:3). Generally, an *-eth* on the end of a word indicates a continuing practice. "He that committ*eth* sin is of the devil" means that he who continues to commit sin is of the devil. So "every man that hath this hope in him purifieth himself" means that he continues to practice a life of purity. No act of impurity is ever justifiable. In looking at the proper expressions of purity, it will hardly be possible to deal with such expressions without using some of the improper expressions discussed earlier in this treatise. The Bible often lists the pure alongside the impure, and repeats its warnings against impurity again and again.

Proper Words

1. Moral purity is expressed in the use of proper words. Words can be sound, edifying, beautiful, clean, and pure, or they can be sensual and devilish.

"Be ye therefore followers of God, as dear children; and walk in love, as Christ also hath loved us, and hath given himself for us an offering and a sacrifice to God for a sweet smelling savour. But fornication, and all uncleanness, or covetousness, let it not be once named among you, as becometh saints; neither filthiness, nor foolish talking, nor jesting, which are not convenient: but rather giving of thanks" (Ephesians 5:1–4). Verse 2 says that Jesus Christ offered Himself to God for a sweet-smelling savor. His life smelled good. An aroma went up to God through the purity and sacrifice of Jesus Christ. The Lamb that was without spot—that is, without any impure words or moral blemishes in His life—offered Himself to God, a sweet-smelling savor. But a different odor goes up from the corrupt practices and from the filthy talk related to moral corruption. "Neither filthiness, nor foolish talking, nor jesting, which are not convenient" does not refer to clean, wholesome humor, but to filthy and foolish jokes particularly about sex. There are a lot of people who do not know how to talk about sex other than in a silly or suggestive manner. One of the

Moral Purity

things that often leads to immoral actions is joking and making light of something that God designed to be sacred. The sexual urges are God-given and are just as normal as hunger urges. They need to be *controlled* in a similar way. Sexual urges are even greater than hunger urges and therefore need even greater control, but in their proper place, they are beautiful and nothing to be making sensual jokes about. Never should any sensual jokes be made about the sexual life. This is what the Ephesian writer is talking about. He continues, "Ye know, that no whoremonger, nor unclean person, nor covetous man . . . hath any inheritance in the kingdom of Christ and of God. Let no man deceive you with vain words: for because of these things cometh the wrath of God upon the children of disobedience. Be not ye therefore partakers with them" (Ephesians 5:5–7). "Covetous man" in this context may refer to persons who are always wanting more sensual corruption. The pleasures of sin never satisfy the heart. Our words are to be right words. Jesus spoke of keeping the speech clean when He said, "Out of the abundance of the heart the mouth speaketh" and "Every idle word that men shall speak, they shall give account thereof in the day of judgment" (Matthew 12:34, 36).

The leader of a traveling group had his niece with

him. She was a grown, attractive, young orphan girl. One day he told the group, "This is my pet." He meant it in a good sense—that she is an orphan girl, and that he was taking good care of her on this trip. Later, as she entered the bus we were traveling in, a man of the group made a remark that may have indicated a filthy condition in his heart. He looked up at the girl and then at the director and said, "May we pet your pet?" Jesus said: "Out of the abundance of the heart the mouth speaketh" (Matthew 12:34). This kind of foolish talking and jesting is probably what Ephesians 5:4 refers to and can quickly lead to moral deterioration and immoral practices.

"Set a watch, O Lord, before my mouth; keep the door of my lips" (Psalm 141:3). "For he that will love life, and see good days, let him refrain his tongue from evil, and his lips that they speak no guile: let him eschew evil, and do good; let him seek peace, and ensue it. For the eyes of the Lord are over the righteous, and his ears are open unto their prayers: but the face of the Lord is against them that do evil" (1 Peter 3:10–12). When people make silly jokes about something that is sacred, we do well to offer a word of rebuke and encourage them to speak properly.

The children of God use words that edify, and help lift people to a higher plane of living. God's ways are always the best. The clean, pure way is the best way, and we are always happier when we take God's way. Jesus said, "Blessed are the pure in heart: for they shall see God" (Matthew 5:8). We learn (if we do not learn it now, we will learn it later) that God's way is always the best way.

Proper Attire

2. Moral purity is expressed in proper attire. In Proverbs 7 where a moral casualty takes place, special mention is made of the attire of an harlot. The Bible speaks much about modest apparel. The immodest apparel and immorality of our day go together. One of the reasons why there is so much moral corruption today is that there is so much immodest dress. And in some cases, immodest dress is intended to stimulate immoral behavior. In fact, the fashion designs of the world are largely intended to develop pride and to stimulate lust.

The Bible teaches that the body should be well covered. This is illustrated in the very first covering that God provided for man. Adam and Eve tried to cover themselves with a very fractional and fragile covering. God provided for them an adequate covering. Adam and Eve made aprons of leaves. God made coats of skins (Genesis 3:7, 21). Now, a coat is an adequate covering. Providing those coats of skins involved the shedding of the blood of innocent creatures. This is a type of Jesus Christ, through whom salvation is provided for us, which makes us acceptable with God. God wants our bodies adequately covered so as to symbolize the sufficiency of the blood of Jesus Christ to provide a garment of salvation, which is acceptable to Him.

Our practice of dressing modestly leaves a testimony with the world. Relating to this, I would like to tell of a happening at a jail service held by one of our churches. There was a young man in jail that the pastor personally spoke to. The young man said, "I would like to know why your girls and young women dress as they do. Why don't they use make-up? Why do they wear a covering on their heads? Why do they wear those long, plain dresses?"

The pastor replied, "Would you tell me what your name is? I would like to converse with you by name."

"Just call me Grasshopper," was his reply.

"But I would like to know your real name," the pastor insisted.

"Just call me Grasshopper," was his second reply.

"All right," the pastor said. "Grasshopper, I'd like to ask you a few questions. Suppose you were out on the street and you met a painted-up, fractionally clad woman—the way they dress themselves in today's society. What do you feel like? How does it affect you?"

The young man hung his head and then said, "Well, I tell you. It makes me feel like—it brings the very worst out of me."

"How does it make you feel, and what do you think of when you see our sisters modestly clothed?" continued the pastor.

Again, he paused a bit and then replied, "It makes me feel as though I'd like to be what I ought to be."

Perhaps there is no more powerful, silent expression of purity and heavenliness, and nothing more beautiful in this world than a modestly clothed, veiled woman. The apostle Paul, when addressing the importance of modest apparel, stresses "which becometh women professing godliness" (1 Timothy 2:10). I do not believe that any ungodly man or woman can look at a modestly clothed, veiled woman wearing modest hosiery, and not be reminded of godliness. One of the important ways to express moral purity is by proper attire.

Sanctified Courtship

3. *Moral purity is expressed in a sanctified courtship.* Courtship is that period of time in the life of a single man and a single woman spent together

studying each other's character and getting acquainted with each other in the interest of sharing in a lifelong marriage union.

Quoting our basic Scripture again, the apostle Paul wrote, "This is the will of God, even your sanctification, that ye should abstain from fornication: that every one of you should know how to possess his vessel in sanctification and honour; not in the lust of concupiscence, even as the Gentiles which know not God" (1 Thessalonians 4:3–5).

This passage demands that Christian courtship should not be tainted with moral corruption "even as the Gentiles [do] which know not God." The Christian will want to come to the marriage altar and possess his marriage partner (vessel) in sanctification and honor.

Some people in the Bible beautifully exemplify the purity of courtship. Joseph and Mary were given in marriage, but were not yet living together,* when an angel told Mary that she would conceive Jesus in her womb. Mary answered right away that this was not humanly possible because she had not yet known a man. The angel assured her that the coming child would be conceived through the Holy Ghost, and not by a human father (Luke 1:26–35). Likewise, when Joseph learned that Mary was to be a mother, his immediate reaction was that her child could not possibly be his. An angel needed to assure him that Mary's conception was of the Holy Ghost and that his intended bride was still a holy and pure virgin (Matthew 1:18–21).

Joseph and Mary kept themselves pure all through this period (Matthew 1:24, 25). They were able to possess each other in honor in their marriage union.

The record of Jacob and Rachel in Genesis indicates clearly that, although they lived together in the same household during a seven-year courtship and engagement period, they kept themselves from any involvement in immoral conduct (Genesis 29:21). They were able to come to their wedding day and possess each other in honor.

One of the outstanding qualities that the Bible portrays about Rebekah, who was to be the wife of the patriarch Isaac, was that she was a beautiful, pure virgin, untainted by moral defilement (Genesis 24:16).

*According to the Jewish custom of the time, after the couple was given in marriage, there was a delay of one year before the husband would bring his wife into his home (the realization of the marriage). During this period, a writ of divorce was necessary if he wanted to abandon his wife (Matthew 1:19).

SOME HELPS TO PURITY

Maturity

There are some helps to purity that young people do well to keep in mind. One is the principle of maturity. The Bible says that a man (not a boy) should leave his father and mother and be joined to his wife (Genesis 2:24). And Paul wrote that the younger women (not young girls) should marry (1 Timothy 5:14).

Marriage too often takes place about the time that courtship should only begin. The records indicate that early courtship and teenage marriages more often end up a casualty than do the more mature courtships and marriages. A good degree of physical, emotional, and spiritual maturity is necessary to cope with the youthful lusts and with the problems and temptations that are common to all of us.

Proper Social Interests

In chapters 13–16 of the Book of Judges, the life and social interests of Samson are recorded, from which we may learn some valuable lessons. Samson had a beautiful beginning in his service for God (Judges 13:25). In his social interests, however, he did not fare very well. He was attracted to a young Philistine woman, doubtless on the basis of her physical charm rather than for her character or spiritual qualities. Physical charm alone will not satisfy for very long.

As Samson went "down" (it was indeed a downward course) to see his charming Philistine friend, a young lion roared against him—probably intending to destroy and devour him. Samson made quick riddance of the lion by killing him barehanded. On a later trip "down," he found a swarm of honeybees and some sweet honey in the lion's carcass. He ate some of the honey and gave some to his parents.

Since a lion roaring after people is a type of the devil roaring after us to destroy us (1 Peter 5:8), this lion may well have symbolized what was happening to Samson socially. A Philistine "social lioness" was roaring after him. Had he conquered himself and slain his passionate interest in this "social lioness" that was after him, as well as her interest in him, life would have been sweeter for him than was the honey from the literal lion that had roared against him, which he had killed.

Samson's interest in this Philistine lioness ended in a social tragedy. On the day of their marriage and "reception," in bitter disappointment with his bride, whose beauty was only skin deep, he called her his heifer (Judges 14:18) and in anger walked away from the reception and went back "up" to his father's house.

Some way, indeed, to end a wedding-day reception! Samson's interest in this woman might fit well the words of the poet who wrote:

"Thou hast no fault, or I no fault can spy;
Thou art all beauty, or all blindness I."

The record says that Samson's parents in their protest to his interest in this woman "knew not that it was of the Lord" (Judges 14:4). The probable meaning of this is that they knew not that God was permitting this friendship and would overrule to frustrate the marriage union, and at the same time overrule in the destruction of some wicked Philistines who were tormenting Israel and were ripe for the judgment of God. The Israelites were commanded in the Law not to make marriages with the heathen (Deuteronomy 7:3). The New Testament says that Christians shall marry "only in the Lord" (1 Corinthians 7:39). If we are to marry only in the Lord, then we must keep our courtship interests only in the Lord.

Samson's social interest that focused on Delilah, another Philistine woman, led him into the binding, blinding, and grinding effects of perverted interests and indiscreet conduct (Judges 16). His course "down" this time involved physical familiarities with Delilah, even to the extent of going to sleep with

Moral Purity

his head on her lap.

Samson's going to sleep physically was symbolic of what was happening to him spiritually. As he played along with the wiles of his "loving" enticer, his supernatural strength from God departed from him and made him an easy victim of his enemies, which were also the enemies of God. They finally were able to bind him, gouge out his eyes (symbolizing his loss of spiritual eyesight through yielding to his enticing lover), and make a grinding, captive slave out of him. Samson gave them an occasion to blaspheme his God and to praise their blind, deaf, lifeless, and power-less god, Dagon, as giving them victory over their enemy, Samson.

Samson was a miraculously strong man and had no idea when he started paying attention to the "woman [down] in the valley of Sorek" that he would be brought to such weakness, sorrow, and shame. But playing along with Delilah's enticements was like taking coals of fire into his bosom, and he got burnt! The longer he went along with her enticements, the weaker his resistance became. The more one plays with sin, the weaker the conscience becomes until it may seem all right to do the thing that is all wrong. After the fall, the conscience often returns again with renewed, smiting power. That smiting conscience is provided by the mercy of God and is intended to lead us to repentance and victory.

Samson is a striking example of gradual, gross failure in his social interests as well as an example of the gracious forgiveness of God for those who return unto Him. In his last recorded words, he cried, "O Lord GOD, remember me" (Judges 16:28). God remembered him in mercy, gave him the greatest victory of his lifetime, and placed his name among the heroes of faith and works in Hebrews 11.

Some Social Life Don'ts

The social-life failures of Samson suggest a few important *don'ts* to keep in mind.

Don't go to the wrong place or to the wrong people for courtship interests.

Don't be attracted primarily by physical charm.

Don't allow momentary attraction to captivate permanent interests.

Don't continue friendship with a friend who entices to wrongdoing.

Don't be confidential with a stranger. It ruined Samson.

Don't engage in physical familiarities. It deadens the conscience to the dangers of disease and death—physical and spiritual.

Moral Purity

Don't fail to repent and call upon God when you have failed.

Don't fail to "keep thy heart with all diligence" and to seek to express purity in the practice of high standards of social and moral purity.

THE BEAUTIFUL SNOW

Oh, the snow! the beautiful snow,
Filling the sky and the earth below!
Over the housetops, over the street,
Over the heads of the people you meet,
>   Dancing—
>   Flirting—
>   Skimming along.
Beautiful snow! it can do no wrong;
Flying to kiss a fair lady's cheek;
Clinging to lips in a frolicsome freak.
Beautiful snow from the heavens above,
Pure as an angel and gentle as love.

Oh, the snow! the beautiful snow!
How the flakes gather and laugh as they go!

Whirling about in its maddening fun,
It plays in its glee with everyone.
      Chasing—
         Laughing—
            Hurrying by,
It lights on the face, and it sparkles the eye;
And e'en the dogs with a bark and a bound
Snap at the crystals that eddy around.
The town is alive, and its heart is aglow
To welcome the coming of the beautiful snow.

How the wild crowd goes swaying along,
Hailing each other with humor and song!
How the gay sleighs like meteors flash by,
Bright for a moment, then lost to the eye.
      Ringing—
         Swinging—
            Dashing they go
Over the crest of the beautiful snow:
Snow so pure when it falls from the sky,
To be trampled in mud by the crowd rushing by;
To be trampled and tracked by the thousands of feet,
Till it blends with the horrible filth in the street.

Once was I pure as the snow, but I fell;
Fell, like the snowflakes from heaven—to hell;

Moral Purity

Fell, to be trampled as filth in the street;
Fell, to be scoffed, to be spit on and beat.
      Pleading—
           Cursing—
                Dreading to die,
Selling my soul to whoever would buy;
Dealing in shame for a morsel of bread,
Hating the living and fearing the dead.
Merciful God! have I fallen so low?
And yet was I once like this beautiful snow?

Once I was fair as the beautiful snow,
With an eye like its crystals, a heart like its glow;
Once I was loved for my innocent grace—
Flattered and sought for the charm of my face.
      Father—
           Mother—
                Sisters—all,
God and myself I have lost by my fall!
The veriest wretch that goes shivering by
Will make a wide sweep lest I wander too nigh;
For of all that is on or about me, I know,
There is nothing that's pure—but the beautiful snow.

How strange it should be that this beautiful snow
Should fall on a sinner with nowhere to go!

Proper Expressions of Purity

How strange it would be, when the night comes again,
If the snow and the ice struck my desperate brain:
    Fainting—
        Freezing—
            Dying alone—
Too wicked for prayer, too weak for my moan
To be heard in the crash of the crazy town
Gone mad in the joy of the snow's coming down—
To lie and to die in my terrible woe,
With a bed and a shroud of the beautiful snow!

Helpless and foul as the trampled snow,
Sinner, despair not! Christ stoopeth low
To rescue the soul that is lost in sin
And raise it to life and enjoyment again.
    Groaning—
        Bleeding—
            Dying for thee,
The Crucified hung on th' accursed tree!
His accents of mercy fall soft on thine ear:
"There is mercy for thee"; He will hear thy weak prayer.
"O God, in the stream that for sinners did flow,
Wash me, and I shall be whiter than snow."

—John W. Watson

Moral Purity

Proper Activities

Many activities can be engaged in during courtship
that will be an aid to moral purity: going to church
together, singing together, studying the Bible together,
memorizing Scripture together, sharing together in
distribution of Gospel literature, visiting relatives
and others—especially older folks, enjoying God's out-
of-doors in various ways.

Those couples who spend their time in physical
contacts and intimacies will bring regrets rather than
happiness. The happiest people in the world are the
purest people. "Blessed [happy] are the pure in heart"
(Matthew 5:8).

We sometimes need to avoid situations and persons in order to maintain purity. Of such situations,
Proverbs 4:15 says, "Avoid it, pass not by it, turn from
it, and pass away." A young man dating whom he
thought was a respectable young lady found himself
in company with one who made suggestive advances
toward him. He rightly bade her farewell and never
dated her again.

One of the early church fathers, who had lived in
moral impurity before being delivered from his past
life, saw someone, with whom he had been involved
in sin, coming toward him on the street. Quickly he
turned and went the other way. She hastened her

pace, and when he realized this, he hastened his pace. He actually began to run, and she called after him, "It is I," and repeated his name. He responded as he kept on running, "Yes, but it is no longer I." The Bible says, "Flee fornication" (1 Corinthians 6:18).

"Flee fornication," Joseph did that too (Genesis 39:7–12). Even though he suffered severely for it, he kept himself pure. His life was a beautiful expression of moral purity.

A Christ-honoring Wedding

4. *Moral purity is expressed in a simple, Christ-honoring wedding.* A simple, beautiful wedding seems to be implied in 1 Thessalonians 4:3–5. The wedding is most God honoring when the marriage partners possess each other on the wedding day in "sanctification and honour." If everything that is designed for lust and pride were taken out of the modern, worldly wedding, there would not be much left.

A wedding service is for the solemn joining of a man and a woman in a lifelong, "one flesh" union. The wedding day is not a time for a foolish and vain display of lust and pride. Frivolous and nonsensical things, such as publicly kissing the bride, jingling glasses, the wedding couple feeding each other cake, rice throwing, decorating cars with crepe paper and

101

signs, attaching rattling things to cars, and driving after the bridal pair in a hilarious way, with horns blowing, are not compatible or consistent with the solemnity and sacredness of marriage. When an outward display of vanity is needed on the wedding day, it is evident that the inner qualities of humility, purity, and true love that contribute to meaningful and lasting relationships are lacking.

The Lord Jesus Christ came all the way from heaven and while here, He attended a wedding in Cana of Galilee (John 2:1–11). We are not told who the bride and groom were, but we *are* told that Jesus was there. He was the pre-eminent one at the wedding. A Christian wedding should be simple enough and pure enough for Jesus to be there and to be the most prominent person of the wedding-day service and activities.

A Legitimate Christian Marriage Relationship

5. *Moral purity is expressed and maintained in a legitimate marriage union—a husband-and-wife relationship.* The Bible says, "Husbands, love your wives" (not someone else's wife) and "Wives, submit yourselves unto your own husbands" (not someone else's husband) (Ephesians 5:22, 25). To love or pay special attention to someone other than one's

marriage partner spoils the beauty and endangers the stability of the marriage union. It is a beautiful expression of moral purity and marital stability when marriage partners live together in an exclusive love relationship for life, be it twenty, forty, or sixty years, or as long as they both shall live. They are indeed a monument to the divine purpose of the permanence of love in the marriage union.

Physical intimacies within the marriage bond have a place in God's plan. The "bone of my bones, and flesh of my flesh" and the "one flesh" descriptions of marriage (Genesis 2:21–25) suggest that marriage is basically a physical union. For this reason, the marriage bond is for only as long as both partners live physically. A second marriage can be had in purity when neither one entering the second marriage has a former companion living physically (Romans 7:2, 3). A God-designed marriage provides a legitimate relationship in which physical intimacies and endearment can find fulfillment in wholesome and pure expressions (Proverbs 5:18–23). This is true of both Christian and non-Christian, one-flesh marriage unions when the partners are properly married. Hebrews 13:4 declares that "marriage is honourable in [all mankind] and the bed undefiled: but whoremongers [those who give themselves over to sexual liberties outside of marriage] and adulterers God will judge."

It should be noted here that physical intimacies in a proper marriage arrangement are wholesome and undefiling, and are the exclusive right of the married. However, they should be enjoyed only in privacy and not displayed in any way before the public or in the presence of children in the home. For married couples to sit closely together in their automobile or to express their physical charm or attraction to each other by holding hands, kissing, or embracing in public is both unethical and damaging to the witness of purity.

It is, however, altogether right for husbands and wives to be courteous to each other. Recently, a young couple who have been married several years and are the parents of several little children were observed walking together. The husband went stomping ahead of his wife, empty-handed, while she, carrying a large handbag and a baby, followed him. He seemed entirely disinterested in being courteous, kind, loving, or helpful to her. He did not act that way before they were married. But now when his courtesy would have really counted, his first love seemed to have left him.

Another man was very courteous to his lady friend before their marriage. After marriage, when his wife was carrying a baby in her arms and a satchel in her hand, and she happened to stumble, he was heard to say, "What is the matter? Are you getting clumsy?"

Such unkindnesses do not belong to Christian husband-and-wife relationships. Though the couple should continue to express unselfishness and to show a loving interest in and consideration for each other, physical intimacies belong only between the two of them in the privacy of their own home.

Procreation Through the Marriage Union

6. *Moral purity is expressed in procreation through the marriage union.* When God created Adam and Eve, He breathed into man's nostrils the breath of life, and man became a living soul. The word *life* here, Hebrew scholars tell us, is used in the plural sense. If life is plural, that could possibly mean "the succession of lives." Every new life through procreation is a part of the original act of God in the creation of that first man and woman.

God has designed that the propagation of the human race should be done through the marriage union. "Marriage is honourable in all, and the bed undefiled" (Hebrews 13:4). This is God's method of propagating the human family in a pure way. When God created man—one male and one female for each other—insofar as the divine record goes, the first commission He gave them was "Be fruitful, and multiply" (Genesis 1:27, 28).

When we think about the miracle of procreation, we cannot help marveling at the wisdom of Almighty God. We are told that the largest of the two cells which unite to begin a new life is two hundred times as large as the smaller cell, and that the larger one weighs only one two-hundred-thousandth of a gram. That is infinitely small. As the new life begins, body cells move in to build that life.

The body cells are so small that it would take five million of them to make a drop of blood the size of a pinhead. They are unintelligent cells (they have no minds of their own), yet they move in there and build a marvelous bodily structure, which also has no intelligence of its own during the building process. The mother body in which the new structure is formed does not give any directions in the building of the new body.

When those little builder cells begin the building process of a new body, some of them build the muscles of the body, some build the bones, some build the joints, some build the heart, and the brain, the eyes, the ears, and the vocal cords. They all build their various parts so perfectly and with such speed that,

106

according to one doctor's information, by the end of thirty days after the beginning of the new life, that little body has increased to eight thousand times the size of its original cell beginning.

Behold! the magnificence, the sacredness, and the miraculousness of procreation. When the new body makes its appearance in this world, it is a body with eyes that can see, ears that can hear, a voice, hands, muscles, and a heart that beats and pumps blood through the body. It has a circulatory system, a respiratory system, a digestive system, and other systems that function automatically. The body is a tremendous system of automation.

Then the intelligence develops. The human mind is simply terrific. Truly, we are "fearfully and wonderfully made" (Psalm 139:14).

This process of procreation should be looked upon as a very sacred trust that God has given to husbands and wives. God's plan for the human family through procreation is that it would reproduce and populate the world as well as increase the population of heaven. He has provided the marriage union so this can be done in moral purity for His honor and glory and for the happiness and blessing of mankind.

The apostle Paul uses the human body to illustrate the concept of the church. "God [has] set the members everyone of them in the body, as it hath pleased him" (1 Corinthians 12:18). Since the cells that build the body have no intelligence and since the mother body makes no mental contribution toward the building of that new body, we must conclude that this new living creature is a product of the wisdom and power of Almighty God. God is indeed the one who has set the members every one of them in our physical bodies as it has pleased Him.

Purity in Infancy and Childhood

When this new child makes its appearance in the world, there are a number of things to be careful about for the sake of moral purity.

One of the first needs of the body is clothing. Man does not come into this world clothed. Along with clothing the new body comes the temptation to make a showpiece out of this new little child that God created and whom we have now brought into the world. These little ones belong to heaven. Jesus said so (Matthew 19:14). They belong to God; so they ought to be clothed in a way that pleases God, not in a way that pleases the world or that pleases the possible carnality or pride of the parents. Sometimes parents who dress simply themselves dress their little children in bright, showy clothes, thus giving expression to possible pride in their hearts. Because this little one belongs to Jesus Christ and to heaven, he should be clothed in godly modesty. Babies and little, growing children do not choose their clothing. Their parents do, and sometimes friends and relatives do by their gifts of clothing. Sometimes parents begin very early to turn their pure, little, innocent children over to the devil, to the world, and to hell. They like to doll up their little ones and then listen with a degree of pride as they hear people say, "Isn't she a little doll?"

Is it not strange how doll manufacturers try to make the dolls look and act and feel as much like human babies as possible, and then parents turn around and want to make their sweet little children look as much like dolls as possible? "Isn't she a doll?" is really no compliment. She is no doll. She is a living soul that belongs to heaven. The baby's clothing should speak of humility and heavenliness, not of pride and worldliness.

Protecting Our Children

Another problem relating to clothing the children is the tendency of only half clothing the body as they develop physically. Little children dressed so as to expose their lower limbs, sometimes as much as halfway to their waists, are simply being prepared to fit into a society whose thoughts are only evil continually. Parents may also unwittingly be making rapist or white-slave bait out of their children by the way they dress them.

A number of years ago in the state of Michigan, a man who was driving along the highway stopped and picked up a little four-year-old girl. The story ended with him murdering that little girl. In his court trial he said a number of times, "I don't know what made me do it. An urge came over me." Yes, we know what that urge was. Why did that urge come over him? Did the little girl's mother contribute to it by how she dressed her child? She might have. Lots of little girls' clothing contributes to that kind of an urge—an unsanctified urge that evil men oftentimes possess and give vent to.

Sexual abuse of children by adults has reached almost epidemic proportions today in America. Parents ought to be warned about letting their children out on the highways or alone in stores. They ought to be sure these little ones look like heavenly beings, not like they belong to the world, the flesh, and the devil and so become targets of rapists or white slavers.

Recently an international, religious periodical

reported the almost unbelievably startling information that "more than one million children are kidnapped or sold into prostitution each year as a part of a multibillion-dollar, international sex racket. . . . Pedophiles are very active and very dangerous in the United States and Europe. They are not old men leering at children on the playground. They are the teachers and youth leaders!"

Statistics are not always correct, but such information does represent corrupt and frightening conditions. May the gracious Lord God protect our children, and may we be careful to have them appear in a way that God can be pleased to protect them.

Teaching Our Children Modesty and Purity

Some time ago several families were visiting together in a home. A tiny, modestly dressed, preschool girl came into the living room where the group was sitting. She attempted to climb up on a chair. As she climbed up and turned around on the chair, she carefully kept her dress down well over her lower limbs. She must have had the right principle instilled into her to perform as she did. Her dress was of sufficient length and fullness so that she could do it modestly.

Moral Purity

That little girl has grown up now, is a member of the church, and is one of the very finest examples of modesty. Little children who are taught and dressed properly learn young that their bodies are sacred and need to be kept well covered to be kept pure. These little children are an invaluable expression of purity.

Another early need of these little ones is nourishment. When the natural means of nourishment is used, modesty should be expressed in this area also. Mother needs to use discretion and reserve when giving the child nourishment.

Another constant need is clean clothes. Reserve and modesty should be practiced when these little ones need changes of clothing. Discretion should be used as to the place and manner of bathing little ones and changing their clothes.

Everybody ought to be familiar with and follow the guidelines in the booklet *Purity in the Christian Home**.

Little children are inquisitive. It is only normal when they inquire about where they came from. The problem is that too often they get their information from vulgar sources.

*Available from Rod and Staff Publishers, Inc.

Giving Teaching and Supervision

Problems of improper speech about moral issues may occur among children in a home, between families, or in our schools. Positive measures need to be employed to correct them. Conditions should be such that along with a reserve relating to the origin of life and the propagation of the race, there ought to be enough liberty and good, wholesome communication between parents and children that children will learn in the home what is holy, right, clean, and pure.

Recently there was a problem in one of our schools that needed attention and correction. Perhaps it would be profitable to share the method that was used in correcting this. A meeting was planned with the fathers of all the children who were reported to have shared things that were considered unwholesome. At this meeting, helpful suggestions were exchanged, and it was decided that a letter should be sent to all the patrons of the school. Part of the letter reads as follows:

We would like to share the following suggestions with all our patrons.

1. Life, and especially the secrets of the origin of life, should be shared with the children in the home in a reserved and very sacred way. In one home, where the sacred approach was

taken, a young boy confided in his parents, "When we talk about these things at home, it seems like something good, but when Andrew talks about it at school, it seems like something dirty." When children get information about the origin and processes of life from other children, an unwholesome and vulgar slant is almost invariably used in a sneaky way. This is due to the perversion of the sinful nature and Satan's efforts to take advantage of it.

Children and early teenagers are too young emotionally to handle unguarded sex information. Parents should speak guardedly and with reserve before the family about any and all the private functions of the body. When it is necessary to share information or discuss needs, it is generally wise for the mother to share privately with the young daughter and the father with the young son. This method itself would be a good example of propriety in discussing the subject. Proper sexual information is of such vital importance to our children that it seems imperative that they be informed in the home by the parents, and that the reproduction information be given in a sacred way before the children have opportunity of receiving this information in an undesirable manner. Furthermore, children should be encouraged to discuss any questions they may have on these matters with their parents rather than with siblings or with peers.

2. Children's interests and activities should be watched very carefully. Children who secure exciting reading material like to share it with others. Sensual books and magazines are sometimes kept out in the barn, under mattresses, or in some other secret place. Keeping our eyes open in the back of the head, and perhaps doing a little spying sometimes, may well be in order for parents.

3. It may be very hazardous for children to play together in isolated places. Boys and girls should not be allowed to play together without adequate supervision. This would include brothers and sisters as well.

One young girl of a generation ago who became a disgraced mother by an older brother, confided in a friend that, as children, they often played "Father" and "Mother" when their parents were away from home. (Perhaps Father and Mother were too indiscreet before their children in their relations with each other.) Doctor and nurse games may also be suggestive or lead to unwholesome play. Children's overnight get-togethers, while they may be perfectly innocent and pure, sometimes have questionable aspects and should be discontinued or perhaps never started.

4. When parents hear of unwholesome speech or conduct involving other people's children, they should use Christian carefulness in sharing the problem. Perhaps the first persons to share it with would be the parents of the offending child. If that is unfruitful, the problem could be shared with an official who is in a position to use corrective measures. When parents exploit or expose problems among those who are not patrons or among those patrons whose children are not involved, it may well constitute a form of gossip. Should we not be as considerate of other parents as we would want them to be of us should our children be the offenders?

5. It would be the part of wisdom never to respond with disgust, outrage, or excitement when our children report unwholesome things about other children. Children sometimes get

a real thrill out of seeing parents react to their tales about other parents' bad children. A calm "We will look into the matter" would be much better for the child and the parent. If the child is telling the truth, he will not feel hurt by such a response; and if he is not telling the truth, he will soon be discouraged in his talebearing.

6. The Bible tells us that "foolishness is bound in the heart of a child; but the rod of correction shall drive it far from him" (Proverbs 22:15). Children are born with the same sinful nature that their parents were born with. If we had not been corrected when we erred, we would doubtless have gone on down the road of sin. Let us unite our efforts in wholesome methods of correction so that unwholesome trends might not keep our children from going up the road to the heights of God's best.

7. In this experience we have been made aware again of the benefits of the Christian school. If our children were in the public school system, all these things and many, many more would be there for them to be involved in, and we might never learn of it; or if we would learn of it, there would probably be no measure of correction possible from a school standpoint.

We invite your most fervent prayer support and every other contribution you can make for the betterment of our Christian school as it seeks to shape and mold souls for God's glory now, and for eternity.

—The Committee

These corrective measures proved to be very fruitful for the glory of God and for the purity of the school setting.

IN CONCLUSION

Revelation 21 describes the eternally pure city of the redeemed ones. It is of pure, transparent gold; nothing that defiles shall enter there. There will be purity in its ultimate—"We shall be like him" (1 John 3:2) and have pure minds and pure bodies "fashioned like unto his glorious body" (Philippians 3:21). A pure fellowship, a pure environment, a pure river of water of life, and pure food will be there. The tree of life, which bears twelve manner of fruit, will be there. Celestial air! No mental, moral, or spiritual pollutions or moral perversions will be there. Every thought, word, and activity will be expressed in the presence of purity.

At the close of the preflood era, in which society in general was characterized morally as "only evil continually," there were some of whom God could testify that they were walking before Him with a perfect heart. God's enabling grace and keeping power was able to save them from the judgment of God that fell "upon the world of the ungodly" (2 Peter 2:5).

In the closing days of the Old Testament era, gross, spiritual darkness covered the earth. Conditions among God's professing people were such that God lamented, "I have seen thine adulteries and thy neighings, the lewdness of thy whoredom, and thine abominations" (Jeremiah 13:27), yet there were some that "feared the LORD [and] spake often one to another: and the LORD hearkened, and heard it, and a book of remembrance was written before him for them that feared the LORD, and that thought upon his name. And they shall be mine, saith the LORD of hosts, in that day when I make up my jewels; and I will spare them, as a man spareth his own son that serveth him" (Malachi 3:16, 17). Spare them from what? From the day "that shall burn as an oven; and all the proud, yea, and all that do wickedly, shall be stubble: and the day that cometh shall burn them up, . . . that it shall leave them neither root nor branch" (Malachi 4:1).

"Burn them up" and "leave them neither root nor branch" means that they will suffer the same kind of judgment as did the people of Sodom and Gomorrah, who were left neither root nor branch when God burned them up: "Giving themselves over to fornication, and going after strange flesh, [they] are set forth for an example, suffering the vengeance of eternal fire" (Jude 7).

"Leave them neither root nor branch" does not mean that they will be annihilated, but that they will 'have no further offspring as they suffer the eternal vengeance of God.

In those days of worldwide corruption and moral perversion among the professed people of God, there were some who feared the Lord, walked before Him in purity, and were a special treasure to Him. Thus, they were spared from His righteous judgment.

For our day: "The grace of God that bringeth salvation [a saving from our sins] hath appeared to all men, teaching us that, denying ungodliness and worldly lusts [like Noah, Joseph, Daniel, and others have done], we should live soberly, righteously, and godly, in this present world; looking for that blessed hope, and the glorious appearing of the great God and our Saviour Jesus Christ; who gave himself for us, that he might redeem us from all iniquity, and purify unto himself a peculiar people, zealous of good works" (Titus 2:11–14).

We are now living in the last days prior to the

coming of Jesus for His purified ones. Paul wrote, "This know also, that in the last days perilous times shall come" (2 Timothy 3:1). No guesswork about it: the last days are dangerous days; among the dangers are men of unholiness, without natural affection, fierce, and who are despisers of those that are good.

In fact, the last days are prophesied to be days of unparalleled wickedness in the earth. Peter and Jude both speak of people living as brute beasts in those things in which they corrupt themselves. See 2 Peter 2:12 and Jude 10.

In the Book of Revelation, chapter 18, the last stage and climax of worldwide luxurious, blasphemous, and immoral living is portrayed. In that setting, a voice comes from heaven, saying, "Come out of her, my people, that ye be not partakers of her sins, and that ye receive not of her plagues" (Revelation 18:4).

For these last perilous, immoral, blasphemous, presumptuous, seductive, and deceptive days, Peter declared that "the Lord knoweth how to deliver the godly out of temptations" (2 Peter 2:9). Jude gave the assurance that He "is able to keep [us] from falling" (Jude 24).

"Blessed are the pure in heart: for they shall see God" (Matthew 5:8).

"Keep thyself pure" (1 Timothy 5:22).

WHITER THAN SNOW

Lord Jesus, I long to be perfectly whole;
I want Thee forever to live in my soul;
Break down ev'ry idol, cast out ev'ry foe;
Now wash me, and I shall be whiter than snow.

Lord Jesus, look down from Thy throne in the skies,
And help me to make a complete sacrifice;
I give up myself, and whatever I know—
Now wash me, and I shall be whiter than snow.

Lord Jesus, for this I most humbly entreat;
I wait, blessed Lord, at Thy crucified feet;
By faith, for my cleansing, I see Thy blood flow—
Now wash me, and I shall be whiter than snow.

Lord Jesus, Thou seest I patiently wait;
Come now, and within me a new heart create;
To those who have sought Thee, Thou never saidst no—
Now wash me, and I shall be whiter than snow.

—James Nicholson